God's Love Affair

The Heart of Lent

INTERACTIVE DEVOTIONAL

God's Love Affair

The Heart of Lent

Liena Apšukrapša

Carpenter's Son Publishing

Acknowledgement

REVEREND DOCTOR MIRIAM M. DIXON

Dearest Mimi, thank you for all your contributions to this book. Your love-relationship with the Trinity is the greatest gift you share with all of us.

Contents

The Fourth Week of Lent

The Fifth Week of Lent

Discovering Resurrection

Note to the Reader

"For God loved the world so much that he gave his one and only Son, so that everyone who believes in him will not perish but have eternal life. God sent his Son into the world not to judge the world, but to save the world through Him" (JOHN 3:16-17 NLT).

You hold in your hands a most remarkable invitation to accompany Jesus into and through the most challenging and difficult stretch of His earthy passage as He prepares Himself for the terrible travail of the cross. The Christian season of Lent, which begins on Ash Wednesday and ends just before Easter Sunday, provides the unique opportunity for us to journey with Jesus so that He does not face His suffering alone. With anointed insight, Liena Apšukrapša helps us to take our place in the story, right there at Jesus' side. We are present as Mary pours expensive perfume over the feet of Jesus. We are there when He washes the feet of His disciples and announces His imminent departure. We stand at the foot of the cross with Mary, the mother of Jesus.

Read slowly. Feel the tension. Watch how Jesus responds to unfolding events. Learn from Him what it looks like to face life's challenges with trusting confidence in the Father's loving, empowering presence. And be assured, your willingness to journey with Jesus is a great gift to Him.

Reverend Miriam M. Dixon

The First Week of Lent

From the Mountaintop into the Valley

Beloved Pilgrim,

Let's start our Lenten journey by climbing a mountain to eyewitness the most splendid phenomenon—Jesus' transfiguration.

What have been the most significant mountaintop experiences in your life? Those moments when you felt close to God, inspired, and called. Maybe it was something beautiful that pierced your heart, or a relationship that left you experiencing something you never knew existed. Or perhaps you received an answer to prayer. Did you want this experience to last forever? God gives us consolations to vitalize our routine and to anchor us for storms of desolation. Like the water that runs down from the mountains to irrigate the valleys, so too our epic spiritual experiences are designed to support us in trials and tribulations. The reinforcement of the transfiguration is equally important to Jesus as it is to His disciples. It is their bread for the road to Calvary.

How can you make the best use of your mountaintop experiences to withstand desolations? Come and explore with me.

Preparing to Reflect .

God is waiting for me, has time for me, and delights being with me. I take a few deep, slow breaths to appreciate His relationship with me and center myself in His presence.

I recall the psalmist's words, "You deserve honesty from the heart; yes, utter sincerity and truthfulness. Oh, give me this wisdom" (Psalm 51:6 TLB).

As I begin my Lenten pilgrimage and today's prayer, I pause and get in touch with my true heart. Am I expectant, weary, sad, distant, or content? I bring my real self before God and welcome what He desires to give me today.

Prayer

Here I am, Lord. You are the potter, I am the clay. Mold me into Your beautiful image. Amen.

Story of the Day

About eight days after Jesus said this, he took Peter, John and James with him and went up onto a mountain to pray. As he was praying, the appearance of his face changed, and his clothes became as bright as a flash of lightning. Two men, Moses and Elijah, appeared in glorious splendor, talking with Jesus. They spoke about his departure, which he was about to bring to fulfillment at Jerusalem. Peter and his companions were very sleepy, but when they became fully awake, they saw his glory and the two men standing with him. As the men were leaving Jesus, Peter said to him, "Master, it is good for us to be here. Let us put up three shelters—one for you, one for Moses and one for Elijah."(He did not know what he was saying.) (Luke 9:28-33).

Entering the Scene

From the beginning of time God laid out the mountains like peaceful sanctuaries for eager pilgrims. The steeples of peaks reaching upward resonate with our longing for God. The journey itself to the mountaintop often becomes a pilgrimage rich in spiritual discoveries. Do mountains entice and lure you?

Jesus had climbed many mountains and hills to commune with His Father in solitude. But this ascent is different. The Spirit moves Jesus to bring three of His closest disciples with Him. This is our Lord's last mountaintop experience before His descent into the valley of death. How long is their journey? What do they talk about as they scale the mountain slope?

Finally, all four of them arrive at the summit. Jesus does not waste any time and immediately begins to pray as His disciples surrender to exhaustion and fall asleep. Can you keep watch with Jesus?

Suddenly you can't believe your own eyes. You see Jesus' face turning radiant. Dazzling rays of light spread far around. You try to protect your eyes, but you can't resist the captivating scene. Waves of white light gush through His clothing. Jesus stands before you like a burning bush in the desert, luminous with uncreated light. How do you react?

Finally, the disciples awaken and struggle to fathom another dreamlike sight. They face not only the transfigured Jesus but two other glowing men. How would you paint their disorientation? How do they come to discern these men to be Moses and Elijah?

Jesus gets absorbed in conversation with the two Old Testament prophets about His death at Jerusalem to be carried out in accordance with God's plan. What do they say to each other? Are Moses and Elijah consoling Jesus and strengthening Him for His upcoming mission? Then the two mighty men of God start to leave.

Peter, seeing their parting, jumps to his feet and blurts out, "Master, this is wonderful! We'll put up three shelters—one for you and one for Moses and one for Elijah!" (Luke 9:33 TLB).

How do you respond to Peter's words?

Going Deeper

Many of us would be drawn to say, "Peter, don't break the moment! Just be. Take in this glorious light and let it transform you." But Peter cannot be in the present; he has to get busy. He can't let the moment pass without wanting to immortalize it.

But there is something important to keep in mind about the mountaintop. It is not a place where we live permanently. Sooner or later we have to engage the challenges of daily living and even desolations.

Have you ever had an epic spiritual experience only to find yourself being attacked by doubt, fear, and discouragement shortly after? It's difficult for the enemy to influence us during consolation, but he will do everything to distract us from the revelation we receive. His intent is always to get us off the path the Father calls us to walk.

When we are in desolation, our sense of hope, love, faith, and God's presence decreases. A combination of disquietude, agitation, boredom, apathy, fear, worry, and secrecy washes over us. How do you deal with this state of being?

Faithful men of God like St. Ignatius advise us to name the experience for what it is, take a stand, and move in the opposite spirit. "In time of desolation one should never make a change, but stand firm and constant in the resolutions and decision which guided him the day before the desolation, or to the decision which he observed in the preceding consolations."[1] It is wise to focus on working through the desolation itself and not change our course. We are invited to remember what God was saying during our mountaintop experience and *do* what we know God is asking us to do even though we feel great uncertainty and even doubt.

It is natural for our spiritual sense of equilibrium and life's circumstances to ebb and flow. The key is to remain peaceful, steadfast, and confident in Jesus' faithful presence on the mountaintops and in the valleys.

Impressions of Jesus' Heart for Your Journey

My child, remind yourself often,
    The LORD is my shepherd, I lack nothing.
    Even though I walk
        through the darkest valley,
    I will fear no evil,
        for you are with me;
    your rod and your staff,
        they comfort me.
    Surely your goodness and love will follow me
        all the days of my life . . .

Psalm 23:1,4,6

Your Response

What challenged and encouraged you in today's reflection? How is the Spirit moving within you? I invite you to express your heart to the Lord in writing.

With love,
Your fellow pilgrim, Liena

Discerning the Living Voice of God

Precious Child of God,

Jesus was our Father's voice of love on this earth. Jesus continues to speak to us through the indwelling Holy Spirit. Nevertheless, it's a challenge to distinguish His voice from our own random thoughts or the swaying influences that surround us.

What have been your specific challenges in this area? Today I invite you to pursue the guidance of the Holy Spirit with me.

Preparing to Reflect

In preparation to pray and reflect, I still myself and find a comfortable position. I let my breathing become calm and easy. Without forcing it, I allow the rhythm of my breath to gradually slow and deepen. Can I become still enough to sense my heartbeat?

I imagine Jesus taking my hand and inviting me to take a walk with Him into the Scripture scene for today. A road leading to new discoveries arises before us.

Prayer

Lord, I pray that You would have an easy way with me. Soften my resistance and increase my eagerness to follow You. Amen.

Story of the Day

While he was speaking, a cloud appeared and covered them, and they were afraid as they entered the cloud. A voice came from the cloud, saying, "This is my Son, whom I have chosen; listen to him." When the voice had spoken, they found that Jesus was alone. The disciples kept this to themselves and did not tell anyone at that time what they had seen (Luke 9:34-36).

Entering the Scene

Have you ever watched a rapidly developing storm cloud? What did you feel as it relentlessly approached? Or maybe you have been in an actual cloud. Was the fog mystifying and almost blinding?

The drama of the transfiguration keeps unfolding with full force. While Peter is still offering to build three shelters, his eye catches a forming cloud stopping him in mid-thought. The Greek word *episkiasei* indicates that the cloud overshadows Peter and his friends in the same way as the Holy Spirit hemmed in Mary when she conceived Jesus. The disciples are caught in "the storm's eye" of the Trinity.

The cloud swarms around Jesus and his friends until all of them are draped with heaven's hidden stillness. Imagine being inside of this cloud where Christ is your only radiating and pulsating light. What's it like to be shot through and through with His sun-like brilliance?

A voice from within a cloud astonishes all. "This is my Son, whom I have chosen; listen to him" (Luke 9:35). What is Father's voice like?

While the Father is still speaking, Moses and Elijah, the iconic representations of the Law and the Prophets, vanish in the background. Jesus, Father's beloved Son, remains standing for He is the fulfillment of all prophecy and law. Take a few moments to be in awe of this sight.

Going Deeper

On the Mount of Transfiguration the Father's invitation to us all is clear. "This is my Son, whom I love; with him I am well pleased. Listen to him!" (Matthew 17:5).

Apparently, hearing the voice of Jesus is *within our reach*! We are not attempting to decode an obscure message from a distant deity. No! We are communicating with the One who created us, who loves us, and who longs to restore a dialogue. Jesus said, "I am the good shepherd; I know my sheep and my sheep know me" (John 10:14). It *is* possible to distinguish the voice of Jesus from all other voices.

The question for us is, *how* do we discern the living voice of God? The answer is deceptively simple. We learn to discern the voice of God by being with Him. We see this in babies. Newborns *learn* to distinguish the voice of their mother from other voices. Jesus explains that the indwelling Holy Spirit will guide us "into all truth" (John 16:13). But to receive this guidance and know that it comes to us from God requires a personal relationship with the indwelling Holy Spirit. The more we familiarize ourselves with His tone and content from reading the Bible, the better we will be able discern His voice. Any new word from Jesus always lines up with what God has already said in Scripture.

Dallas Willard in his book, *Hearing God,* names several distinguishing factors in discerning the voice of God: the *quality* of the voice of God, the *spirit* of the voice of God, and the *content* of the voice of God.[2]

What is the *quality* of the voice of God? "When Jesus spoke, his words had a weight of authority that opened up the understanding of His hearers."[3] The Lord's voice inspires confidence and gives internal reassurance of truthfulness and rightness. Have you ever felt a qualitative difference between a flash of divine insight and the parochial ideas that characterize your own patterns of thought? "The inner voice of God does not argue, does not try to convince you. It just speaks and it is self-authenticating. It has the *feel* of the voice of God within it."[4] Jesus teaches us with loving authority (Matthew 7:29).

The second distinguishing factor is the *spirit* of God's voice. "It is a spirit of exalted peacefulness and confidence, of joy, of sweet reasonableness and of goodwill."[5]

When I am trying to discern God's voice, I often ask myself, "Do I feel drawn or driven?" The first movement points to the work of the Holy Spirit. God's voice is not an urgent, demanding voice. If a voice is agitated and urgent, suspect the source to be someone or something other than the Lord. God's voice is embodied in Jesus and the caring way He lived His life. James writes, "But the wisdom that comes from heaven is first of all pure; then peace-loving, considered, submissive, full of mercy and good fruit, impartial and sincere" (James 3:17).

A third distinguishing factor concerns the *content* of the message. What information does the voice convey? There are times when God reveals to us areas of our lives that are not aligned with His heart. While the message is not always comfortable, it is never shaming. God's revelation comes more as a "knock" than an intrusion. Jesus asks if I am *willing* to acknowledge the condition, and if I am *willing* to invite His assistance in pursuing my highest good to reflect His glory. Jesus always asks and entices, never forces or demands.

Hearing God's voice might sound a bit complicated, but in practice it flows quite naturally. Remember that the Holy Spirit is dedicated to be your Teacher. If you are truly willing and curious, Jesus will speak into your heart. "Here I am! I stand at the door and knock. If anyone hears my voice and opens the door, I will come in" (Revelation 3:20).

Impressions of Jesus' Heart for Your Journey

My beloved, meet every day with the expectation that I will speak to you. Have faith in My desire to guide you, affirm you, and equip you with wisdom. Affirm and renew your dedication to pay attention to Me.

"The Sovereign LORD has given me an instructed tongue,
to know the word that sustains the weary.
He wakens me morning by morning,
wakens my ear to listen like one being instructed.
The Sovereign LORD has opened my ears;
I have not been rebellious,
I have not turned away."

Isaiah 50:4-5

Your Response

How was your spirit stirred in today's reflection? Respond to the Lord through prayer or journaling.

Grace be with you,
Liena

Christ in You, the Hope of Glory

Dear Friend,

Jesus and His disciples have come down from the Mount of Transfiguration into the valley. In anticipation of His death, our Lord becomes very intentional about preparing the beloved disciples for His departure. Jesus, like any loving person who is to die soon, instills the most important lessons into His disciples' souls.

Are you ready to join His disciples in hearing Jesus' heart? We will spend the next several days unpacking Jesus' words of inheritance for you and me.

Preparing to Reflect

As I ready myself to pray and reflect, I remind myself that I have the authority and ability to create stillness. "If I were a doctor," said the Danish philosopher Søren Kierkegaard, "and were asked for my advice, I should reply, 'Create silence'"[6]

I settle down into my prayer spot and gently remind my soul, "For God alone, O my soul, wait in silence, for my hope is from him" (Psalm 62:5 ESV). I breathe slower and deeper as I repeat this verse several times.

Prayer

"Speak, LORD, for your servant is listening" (1 Samuel 3:9). Amen.

Story of the Day

"I did not tell you this from the beginning because I was with you, but now I am going to him who sent me. None of you asks me, 'Where are you going?' Rather, you are filled with grief because I have said these

things. But very truly I tell you, it is for your good that I am going away. Unless I go away, the Advocate will not come to you; but if I go, I will send him to you" (John 16:5-7).

"If you love me, keep my commands. And I will ask the Father, and he will give you another advocate to help you and be with you forever— the Spirit of truth. The world cannot accept him, because it neither sees him nor knows him. But you know him, for he lives with you and will be in you. I will not leave you as orphans; I will come to you" (John 14:15-18).

Entering the Scene

Downcast and puzzled, the disciples continue listening to Jesus. The Lord's words sound so somber. He is leaving them! This realization is soul-wrenching. No questions asked. The anticipation of grief seizes their hearts and they slip into denial. Can you relate? Would you say anything to Jesus in this situation?

Jesus reads His disciples' grief well. He puts all His energy into giving a context for His departure and with it hope. The Lord assures them that His presence will be more real in their lives after His glorification than now. Jesus will not only be with them, but He will be in them—actually living His divine life through them.

How are the disciples taking Jesus' words? Does Jesus' promise sound too mysterious and even bewildering? Stay for a minute with them as they ponder what this truly means.

Going Deeper

Jesus says that it is for the disciples' good that He leaves. How is this so? Jesus' fellowship with His disciples has always been subjected to interruptions and misunderstandings. Many limitations have affected Jesus' communion with them. Despite Jesus' brilliant teachings, the disciples often have missed His point. The reason has been simple: He has spoken *to* them but not from *within* them.

Jesus promises that this will change when the Holy Spirit comes. Through the Holy Spirit Jesus will live in them permanently, influencing and teaching them from *within*. Jesus is next to them but never in them until the day of Pentecost. "And this is the secret: Christ lives in you. This gives you assurance of sharing his glory" (Colossians 1:27 NLT).

We are living in the most privileged of all times. "In the Old Testament we have the Spirit of God coming upon people and working in them in special times and ways: working from above, without, and within. In the New Testament we have the Holy Spirit entering them and dwelling within them: working from within, without, and upward."[7] Have you experienced this in your life?

We all have the fullness of the Spirit. We don't have to beg Him to come; He is already here. Our part is to be *aware, grateful,* and *responsive.* Many times, I remind my patients in the hospital, "No matter how unwell you feel mentally and physically, *there is a holy and healthy place within you*—the place where the Holy Spirit dwells. He is never broken. Rely on His life to well up within you for strength, healing, and peace."

Now I invite you to take a moment to have a deliberate conversation with the Holy Spirit. Turn your attention inwardly toward the holy of holies where He indwells you. Thank the Holy Spirit for any specific gifts He bestows on you and for any comfort and counsel you receive from Him daily.

Impressions of Jesus' Heart for Your Journey

"If anyone loves me, he will obey my teaching. My Father will love them, and we will come to them and make our home with them" (John 14:23).

My child, you are My favorite dwelling place. I am delighted when you welcome Me and My Father through the indwelling of the Holy Spirit.

Your Response

What are your desires for your relationship with the Holy Spirit? Express them in a verbal prayer or in journaling.

May the Lord bless you,
Liena

The Gift of Absence

Dear Pilgrim,

Have you ever experienced the paradox of feeling someone's presence more in their absence than when they are with you? Your appreciation grows and so does your longing for the one you love.

Jesus continues to assure His disciples that this dynamic will be true in their lives after His departure. Our Lord promises that the indwelling Holy Spirit, *His Spirit,* will reveal to them heavenly mysteries and wisdom that their hearts are not ready to bear in His presence. "Thus, not only our presence but also our absence becomes a gift to others."[8]

Come and discover the gift of absence with me.

Preparing to Reflect

As I come to commune with my loving God, I center down. I am at rest, yet alert. I savor a few deep breaths and use my God-given imagination to paint each word in the following scene:

Christ shield me today . . .

Christ with me, Christ before me, Christ behind me,

Christ in me, Christ beneath me, Christ above me,

Christ on my right, Christ on my left,

Christ when I lie down, Christ when I sit down, Christ in the heart of every man who thinks of me,

Christ in the mouth of everyone who speaks of me,

Christ in the eye that sees me,

Christ in the ear that hears me.

St. Patrick[9]

I stay with this image for few minutes and appreciate Jesus hemming me in.

Prayer

You hem me in behind and before . . .
Such knowledge is too wonderful for me,
   too lofty for me to attain.
                              Psalm 139:5-6

I thank You for heaven's embrace. Amen.

Story of the Day

*"I have much more to say to you, more than you can now bear. But when
he, the Spirit of truth, comes, he will guide you into all the truth. He will
not speak on his own; he will speak only what he hears, and he will tell
you what is yet to come. He will glorify me because it is from me that
he will receive what he will make known to you. All that belongs to the
Father is mine. That is why I said the Spirit will receive from me what he
will make known to you"* (John 16:12-16).

Entering the Scene

Jesus burns with desire to share the mysteries of heaven with His disciples, but His student's limited capacity to receive stops Him. Picture
this moment. The followers of Jesus understanding has reached the
limit. If you are a teacher, you can identify with the Lord. Jesus understands His disciples and promises His further revelation. "I still have
many things to tell you, but you can't handle them now. But when the
Friend comes, the Spirit of the Truth, he will take you by the hand and
guide you into all the truth there is" (John 16:12-13 MSG). The truth
of God cannot be understood without the Spirit of truth. "The Spirit
brings with Him the truth, and then having possessed us from within,
guides us, as we can grasp it, into all truth."[10]

Even further, Jesus assures that the Spirit will not speak in His
own authority but will reveal what He receives from the Son and the
Father. In the life of the Trinity there is nothing more beautiful than
divine equality, teachability, and *ongoing humility to honor each other.*
Can you sense this in Jesus' words?

The Trinity imparts these characteristics in the hearts of the faithful. "This is the disposition He effects in those who truly receive Him: a gentle teachableness that marks the humble in spirit who have come to realize that as worthless as their own righteousness is, so is their wisdom or power to grasp spiritual truth. They acknowledge that they need Christ as much for the one as for the other and that the Spirit within them alone is the Spirit of truth."[11]

Going Deeper

I will never forget the day when I called my friend after a hurtful and upsetting conversation with a person in my life. Through my sobbing I confessed, "He said this and that about me."

My friend asked only one question. "Is it true?"

"No!" I replied.

"Why are you crying then?" she asked.

I stopped.

That day taught me a spiritual discipline of stopping when I feel offended, caught up in emotions, confused, or off balance. I quiet myself and simply ask my best friend, the Holy Spirit, "What is the truth right now?" I listen and let Him tell me what is true about myself, my circumstance, God, and others. If I know the truth, I usually can find my way. And Jesus promises that the Holy Spirit will guide me into all the truth.

It is important to note that many times the Spirit's leading does not involve a change in my circumstances. I still have the same conditions, but He gives me the ability to come at my circumstances from a fresh angle, with a greater depth of field, and with a different mind-set.

When the Holy Spirit speaks truth into your life, what do you notice about the way He speaks to you? The Holy Spirit is always consistent in His approach. He is firm, but never condemning. He is truthful, but never discouraging or shaming. He suggests, but He never demands. His voice is gentle, peaceful, joyful, enthusiastic, assuring, and encouraging.

Part of living an authentic life under the guidance of the Holy

Spirit is learning to speak His language to ourselves and to others. If we want to be united with the Holy Spirit, if we want to walk in cadence with Him, *we cannot afford to have any other conversations with ourselves than the ones He is having with us.* If we do, we cultivate spiritual schizophrenia. We create internal disharmony, jolting, harshness, misalignment, and lack of progress in our lives with the Holy Spirit. Learn heaven's language of compassion that always leads into deeper understanding!

Is your self-talk aligned with the tone of the Holy Spirit? What changes do you want to pursue?

The daily occupation of the Holy Spirit is to lead us into all truth. Jesus, through the Holy Spirit, continues to be our good, loving, and true Shepherd as much in His absence as in His physical presence on this earth.

Impressions of Jesus' Heart for Your Journey

You are precious to Me. I gave you the Holy Spirit to guide you in your every step. My desire for you is deep friendship with Him.

"Since this is the kind of life we have chosen, the life of the Spirit, let us make sure that we do not just hold it as an idea in our heads or a sentiment in our hearts, but work out its implications in every detail of our lives" (Galatians 5:25 MSG).

Your Response

What is your internal reaction to today's reflection? Is the Lord touching your heart in any specific way?

With blessing,
Liena

_____

_____

_____

_____

_____

_____

_____

_____

_____

_____

_____

_____

_____

_____

_____

_____

_____

_____

_____

_____

_____

_____

_____

_____

_____

_____

_____

Abiding in Jesus

God's Beloved,

"I will go so far as to say that the more you can connect, the more of a saint you are."[12] Our oneness with the Trinity and each other is what truly matters. In today's Scripture Jesus speaks about the beauty of connection. The Lord teaches His disciples about abiding in Him even in His absence from this world.

How strongly connected do you feel to Jesus, to the people around you, to your own deepest self? Is there any disconnect in your life that concerns you right now? Let Him address your worries and desires today.

Preparing to Reflect

I settle down and recollect myself before God. I pay attention to my body. Is there any tension? I breathe deeply for a few minutes to release it. Are there any anxious thoughts within me? I gently dismiss them for the time being as Jesus dismissed crowds to seek His Father in solitude. I slowly turn my attention to the Lord who wants to commune with me.

"To pray means to wait for the God who comes. . . . He comes even in moments when we have done everything wrong, when we have done nothing . . . when we have sinned."[13]

Prayer

Father, Son, and Holy Spirit, give me the grace to abide in You as You abide me. Amen.

Story of the Day

"I am the true vine, and my Father is the gardener. He cuts off every branch in me that bears no fruit, while every branch that does bear fruit he prunes so that it will be even more fruitful. You are already clean because of the word I have spoken to you. Remain in me, as I also remain in you. No branch can bear fruit by itself; it must remain in the vine. Neither can you bear fruit unless you remain in me."

"As the Father has loved me, so have I loved you. Now remain in my love. If you keep my commands, you will remain in my love, just as I have kept my Father's commands and remain in his love. I have told you this so that my joy may be in you and that your joy may be complete. My command is this: Love each other as I have loved you. Greater love has no one than this: to lay down one's life for one's friends. You are my friends if you do what I command. I no longer call you servants, because a servant does not know his master's business. Instead, I have called you friends, for everything that I learned from my Father I have made known to you. You did not choose me, but I chose you and appointed you so that you might go and bear fruit—fruit that will last—and so that whatever you ask in my name the Father will give you. This is my command: Love each other" (John 15:1-4, 9-17).

Entering the Scene

Jesus paints a very familiar scene for His disciples, something they can relate to so well. In their homeland the slopes and plains are richly covered with the growth of vines.

It's like Jesus is retelling an old story with new meaning. His Father is an intentional and loving Gardener who planted Jesus in the soil of this earth. And the Holy Spirit is the life-giving Sap flowing through all natural and grafted branches.

How do you relate to the story Jesus is telling? Have you ever grown vines, grafted them, and pruned them?

As a child, I used to help my mother graft branches on existing trees and later prune them. While doing so, I learned striking analogies about our lives in Christ.

The sharp knife makes a deep wound into the heartwood of the tree to make a space for the new branch. Likewise, Christ's feet and hands are pierced with nails for our sake. The Gardener cuts off the branch from a fruitless tree and grafts it onto the good tree. Similarly, the Father cuts us off from our old life that produced the bitter fruit of selfishness and connects us to Jesus. "For you have died, and your life is hidden with Christ in God" (Colossians 3:3 ESV). This change enables us to produce the sweet fruit of the Holy Spirit.

The newly grafted branch only "takes" if the connection to the receiving tree is clean and very tight. The gardener avoids any looseness and gaps in the connection by tying the branch to the tree. Later the grower prunes the branch of false and diseased shoots, opening up a space for the good branch to thrive and grow.

Pruning in the spiritual sense simplifies life and directs concentrated energy in the most beneficial direction. Abundant fruitfulness is the result.

Going Deeper

The story of branch-life is very progressive and unfolds the meaning of life with Christ. Four words characterize the life of deep abiding in Jesus: *enjoying, resting, allowing,* and *loving.*

What does the branch have to do? The branch is absolutely reliant on the vine for everything. The vine does all the work, and the branch simply relishes the connection that produces the fruit. When the Father grafts us to Jesus, He gives us a position of rest.

How do you use your position as a branch to say *no* to fear, panic, anxiety, and worry?

This place of rest is never apathetic and passive. "To abide means to stay in a given place of relationship and expectancy. We don't abide casually. We abide with focus, passion, and a sense of expectancy."[14]

The branches actively receive the nourishment of the vine as it puts forth great effort. It sends its roots out into the dirt and hunts for sustenance. The stem turns what it finds into life-giving sap that then produces the fruit.

Jesus earns and accomplishes everything for us, including the Holy Spirit. The Spirit, our holy Sap, sustains the very life within us through warm summer days and cold winter seasons when there is no appearance of life whatsoever. The Holy Spirit maintains our permanent linkage with Jesus at all times. "The relationship between the vine and the branches is such that the living connection is maintained hourly, daily, unceasingly. The sap does not flow for a time, then stop, and then flow again. Instead, moment to moment, the sap flows from the vine to the branches."[15]

Are you aware of the flow of the Holy Spirit within you? How do you respond to and partner with Him?

Allowing the flow of the Holy Spirit is a core discipline of the Christian life. We develop a compassionate awareness of the heart attitudes that block the movement of the Holy Spirit: the withholding of love and forgiveness, holding onto victimhood and bitterness, hardening our heart, choosing to remain isolated, and being non-receptive. These habits of thought interfere with the flow of the Trinity and our communion with other branches. Cynthia Bourgeault points out that these attitudes reinforce our small, egocentric and self-sufficient existence. "In any situation in life, confronted by outer threat or opportunity, you can notice yourself responding inwardly in one of two ways. Either you will brace, harden, and resist, or you will soften, open, and yield."[16]

It takes courage and commitment to yield to the flow of the Holy Spirit. There are times we would rather hide and shut down. Take a moment to examine your life. Are you called to address any disrupted flow in your relationship with God and others?

Jesus ends His teaching on branch-life with this stunning conclusion. When you love and let the Holy Spirit produce fruit in you, the Father will answer your prayers. "You did not choose me, but I chose you and appointed you so that you might go and bear fruit—fruit that will last—and so that whatever you ask in my name the Father will give you. This my command: Love each other" (John 15:16-17).

Abiding in Jesus means loving like Him. How are you invited not only to pray harder but to love deeper?

Impressions of Jesus' Heart for Your Journey

My friend, I am the Vine and you are My branch. My Father specifically chose you to be grafted into Me. You are My gift from the Father. Rejoice, give thanks, appreciate, and celebrate your branch-life. "Guard, through the Holy Spirit who dwells in us, the treasure which has been entrusted to you" (2 Timothy 1:14 NASB).

Your Response

What desires arise within you as the result of today's time in prayer and reflection?

Father wants to hear your heart and bless you.

With thanksgiving for you,
Liena

Are You an Overcomer?

My Dear Friend,

Who in your life would you consider an overcomer in Christ? What makes them an overcomer? Is it just their willpower, or is there a connection between their victories and deep abiding in Jesus, the True Vine?

In today's Scripture Jesus gives a fair warning to His disciples that there will be many troubles in this world after His departure. But He also says that everything and anything can be overcome if His followers live out His victory in their own lives.

Do you desire to become an overcomer with Jesus? Come alongside me and let's explore the strength of Jesus' heart.

Preparing to Reflect

As I am about to pray, I might make a cup of tea for myself to relax and become calm. With each sip of tea I take, I appreciate the gift of cultivating my relationship with the Lord in this quiet space.

"Silence is not merely negative—a pause between words, a temporary cessation of speech—but, properly understood, it is highly positive: an attitude of attentive alertness, of vigilance, and above all of listening. The hesychast, the person who has attained hesychia, inner stillness or silence, is par excellence the one who listens. He listens to the voice of prayer in his own heart, and he understands that this voice is not his own but that of Another speaking within him."[17]

Prayer

God of goodness,
give me yourself.

You are enough for me.
I can ask for nothing less,
for then I would not be worshiping you.
And if I ask for anything less,
I will always be left wanting.
Only in You
do I have everything.

Prayer by Julian of Norwich[18]

Story of the Day

"I came from the Father and entered the world; now I am leaving the world and going back to the Father."

"A time is coming and in fact has come when you will be scattered, each to your own home. You will leave me all alone. Yet I am not alone, for my Father is with me.

"I have told you these things, so that in me you may have peace. In this world you will have trouble. But take heart! I have overcome the world" (John 16:28, 32-33).

Entering the Scene

Place yourself among Jesus' disciples as His steady gaze and weighty message captures their attention, "I know all things. I know you will flee for your own lives when I am arrested. You will desert me. But do not despair in the face of your own weakness. The world shall not overcome you no matter how severely it tries you because I have prevailed and overcome its dominion."

What is your reaction to Jesus' disclosure? Someone among you might be brave enough to speak up. "Wait a minute, Jesus! Have you really overcome the world? Your greatest battle is still ahead of You. Your enemy, death, is about to devour You. What makes You say these words?"

Jesus' response hushes all into wonder, "My victory is already guaranteed because the Father is with me." How firm must be our Lord's grip on His Father's great love for Him to make the future already a present certainty! "Jesus trusted in the power of the Father to keep Him. It was His reality. His confidence in the Holy Spirit to fill in the gaps after He's gone was absolute. It was so real, that He spoke about the future as the present. He spoke in the language of the Overcomer—from the perspective of heaven on earth."[19]

How does Jesus' assurance of victory move you?

Going Deeper

I often wear a cross that someone made for me many years ago. The arms of this cross stretch out in a victorious and worshipful position. This cross depicts the truth of Jesus being slaughtered and victorious at the same time. What does it take to be a triumphant victim? What is the key to Jesus-like victory in our lives?

This question takes us back to the story of Jesus—the True Vine, the Father—the Great Gardener, and the Spirit—the Holy Sap. Jesus overcomes the world because He moves in the Spirit opposite to the spirit of this world. Every step He takes on the road of Calvary, and every breath He takes on the Cross, He does in the strength of the Holy Sap flowing within Him. Throughout His suffering, our Lord, without fail, moves in the Spirit of love, joy, peace, forbearance, kindness, goodness, faithfulness, gentleness, and self-control. He overcomes the world by *surrendering* to the Father and being *completely aligned* with the fruit of the Spirit. The devil and the world is powerless against such unifying strength. Any move Jesus might have made in a spirit of retaliation, hate, and vengeance would have assured His defeat.

When we abide in Jesus like a branch on a vine, His nature gives us victory over the enemy and the trials of this world.

The fruit of the Spirit is an encounter with God that leads us into an ongoing experience which opens us up to the fullness of who God is for us and becomes the lifestyle that He takes the greatest pleasure in. What God is offering us is His unchanging self so that we, too, can become unchanging in our way of life. That means unchanging in our nature and our character, unchanging in the sense of, "I am going to become like Jesus no matter what occurs, and I am unchanging in that desire." We become constant and consistent in our approach to people and circumstances regardless of whether those are good, bad or ugly. The fruit of the Spirit gives us confidence in His relationship with us, and as we commit ourselves to practicing the fruit of the Spirit what we are doing is we are sewing into His character and reaping back from His favor. Nothing can separate us from the love of God so the fruit of the Spirit is where we learn to abide in God's nature. The fruit of the Spirit is the power of God to enable us to become Christ-like.[20]

How has God taught you to be victorious through practicing the fruit of the Spirit?

My first lesson in this took place when I was fifteen years old. I just had become a friend of Jesus. In my class there was a girl who struggled with attendance. I missed her and was worried about her. One day I decided to walk to my friend's home where she lived with her mother and grandmother.

I knocked on the door, and an unpleasant voice grudgingly welcomed me. My friend's grandmother stood there with her arms tightly crossed and her disapproving eyes looking me up and down. I explained the reason for my visit. Her reply was harsh. "You can visit my granddaughter, but I will sit in the doorway and listen to your conversation."

I quietly greeted my friend and asked how she was doing. Suddenly, as we were talking, the grandmother started to yell at me. "Out of my house. That's enough. Get out of my house!"

As I passed her in the doorway, I felt a wave of the Holy Spirit move right through me. The weight of His love for this woman pressed me to the ground. I knelt before her, put my head in her lap, and hugged her knees. She gasped in disbelief and let out a loud sob. Through streams of tears she told me that she had not been letting my friend attend school because there had been an attempted rape. I assured her of my loyal friendship for her granddaughter and left quietly.

I felt disoriented as I closed the gate to the house. "What just happened?" I asked God.

I heard His gentle reply in my heart. "I am teaching you how to be an overcomer."

My friend returned to school the next day.

Impressions of Jesus' Heart for Your Journey

My beloved, here is a secret to an overcoming life: pray in My name and move in My Spirit. Never let those two be separated. They work as one. Always remember, "the one who is in you is greater than the one who is in the world" (1 John 4:4).

Your Response

What was the most personal message to you from Jesus today? How does this move you to pray now?

Be strong in Him,
Liena

_____

_____

_____

_____

_____

_____

_____

_____

_____

_____

_____

_____

_____

_____

_____

_____

_____

_____

_____

_____

_____

_____

_____

Fellowship in Suffering

Dear Fellow Traveler,

We probably both have heard sermons that indicate following Jesus makes life easier. But does it? Yes, Jesus promises the Spirit-led life. But that does not equate to personal security and luxury. Drawing close to God is to enroll in a difficult school where character is built out of persevering through difficult times. Perseverance creates *resilience*, and resilience leads us into *unfathomable freedom* and an ever-increasing territory of godly influence. Resiliency gives us a genuine authority to speak into other lives.

James writes, "Dear brothers and sisters, when troubles come your way, consider it an opportunity for great joy. For you know that when your faith is tested, your endurance has a chance to grow. So let it grow, for when your endurance is fully developed, you will be perfect and complete, needing nothing" (James 1:2-4 NLT).

Do you want to be ready for anything? Let's explore this path together.

Preparing to Reflect

To pray is to enter the fellowship of all believers of all times. The Holy Trinity is the Host of this sacred gathering and feast. Prayer leads us from loneliness into fellowship.

"When you are praying alone, and your spirit is dejected, and you are wearied and oppressed by your loneliness, remember then, as always, that God the Trinity looks upon you with eyes brighter than the sun; also all the angels, your own Guardian Angel, and all the Saints of God. Truly they do; for they are all one in God, and where God is, there are they also. Where the sun is, thither also are directed all its rays. Try to understand what this means."[21]

As I settle down for my prayer time, I take a moment to appreciate the presence of the Holy Trinity, the angels, and "the great cloud of witnesses" (Hebrews 12:1) surrounding me. I give thanks that I am not alone in the battlefield of life and prayer.

Prayer

Lord Jesus, together with all Your saints I lift up my heart to praise Your glorious and victorious name.

"'Holy, holy, holy is the Lord God Almighty,' who was, and is, and is to come. Worthy is the Lamb, who was slain, to receive power and wealth and wisdom and strength and honor and glory and praise!" (Revelation 4:8; 5:12). Amen.

Story of the Day

"If the world hates you, keep in mind that it hated me first. If you belonged to the world, it would love you as its own. As it is, you do not belong to the world, but I have chosen you out of the world. That is why the world hates you. Remember what I told you: 'A servant is not greater than his master.' If they persecuted me, they will persecute you also. If they obeyed my teaching, they will obey yours also. They will treat you this way because of my name, for they do not know the one who sent me. If I had not come and spoken to them, they would not be guilty of sin; but now they have no excuse for their sin. Whoever hates me hates my Father as well. If I had not done among them the works no one else did, they would not be guilty of sin. As it is, they have seen, and yet they have hated both me and my Father. But this is to fulfill what is written in their Law: 'They hated me without reason.'

"When the Advocate comes, whom I will send to you from the Father—the Spirit of truth who goes out from the Father—he will testify about me. And you also must testify, for you have been with me from the beginning" (John 15:18-27).

Entering the Scene

As a hospital chaplain, I regularly prepare families to see their loves ones in horrific states after car crashes and other traumas. To soften the shock as much as possible, I explain to them what they will see. Jesus does something similar in today's scene.

Jesus warns His disciples about a guaranteed opposition that is on its way. By giving them this warning, He protects them from delusion and confusion.

Place yourself among Jesus' disciples. What do you experience in your spirit as Jesus relays this message? What is the feel of the atmosphere surrounding all of you?

Jesus is very clear with His disciples that this suffering and opposition will come not because of their faults but *precisely* because they are good and belong to a good God. Jesus is clear that the Spirit of God within them will intimidate the evil spirit of this world. "For our struggle is not against flesh and blood, but against the rulers, against the authorities, against the powers of this dark world and against the spiritual forces of evil in the heavenly realms" (Ephesians 6:12). The battle takes place in the heavenly realms but materializes on the earth. The evil one cannot touch the Father, but in his cowardice he uses those on the earth who have strayed from God to attack His faithful children.

Going Deeper

I grew up in Latvia under the occupation of the Soviet Union. My family and I experienced the cowardly tactics of evil firsthand. My mother was born during the Second World War. The evil ran rampant in our country long after the war was over. The country was infiltrated with people who did not know anything about God and were easy targets for the devil to mobilize against the Christians.

I will share a few facts just to give you some perspective on the suffering my fellow Latvians underwent. Our population in 1939, just before the War began, was under two million in the entire country. We lost approximately four hundred thousand people to death in the war zones, and then close to one hundred thousand innocent men, women, and children were sent to Siberian concentration camps after the war.[22] "The victims were gathered in more than 50 assembly points and carted away in more than 600 railway carriages—many nothing but cattle cars with a hole in the corner for bodily functions."[23] The main criteria for these forced deportations were: good education, wealth, oppositional political views, or faith. The Soviets did everything to eliminate any potential opposition and influence.

When my mother was in elementary school, my grandmother gave her a sack of dried bread and a *goodbye forever* kiss each weekday morning. My grandmother was prepared that her daughter could be taken from the school and never seen again. (In deportations children were separated from their parents). They lived with this fear for years.

Just recently I heard a well-known story about a priest in Latvia. It was a crime to possess a Bible. A priest named Victors was arrested for having one. The Soviet agent threw the Holy Scriptures on the floor, right in the front of the priest and asked the priest to step on it. Instead the priest knelt down and kissed the book. For doing this he was condemned to ten years of hard labor in Siberia. One of the first things that Victors did after returning from his tortures was to step out in front of his parish, read aloud the gospel, and declare in a booming voice, while holding aloft the Holy Scriptures, "The Word of God!" The entire church cried in silence but could not applaud him for fear of causing another provocation. That's perseverance with joy. For Victors, the only thing worth living for was his friendship with Jesus, which he reflected wherever he went.

"Now thanks be to God who always leads us in triumph in Christ, and through us diffuses the fragrance of His knowledge in every place" (2 Corinthians 2:14, NKJV).

The more faith is resisted, the more it spreads. It is through discomfort that we learn to persevere and to press on. People carefully listen to the words of men and women who have proven their love for Jesus and demonstrate the strength that comes from Him under the fires of persecution. Their territory and influence ever increases.

"And what more shall I say? I do not have time to tell about Gideon, Barak, Samson and Jephthah, about David and Samuel and the prophets, who through faith conquered kingdoms, administered justice, and gained what was promised; who shut the mouths of lions, quenched the fury of the flames, and escaped the edge of the sword; whose weakness was turned to strength; and who became powerful in battle and routed foreign armies" (Hebrews 11:32-34). Yes, we *become powerful in the battle!*

Impressions of Jesus' Heart for Your Journey

My child, when you suffer for Me, you suffer with Me. Afflictions are the doorway to your union with the Trinity. See the opportunity through My servant Paul's eyes. "And I continually long to know the wonders of Jesus more fully and to experience the overflowing power of his resurrection working in me. I will be one with him in his sufferings and I will be one with him in his death. Only then will I be able to experience complete oneness with him in his resurrection from the realm of death" (Philippians 3:10-11 TPT).

Your Response

Where in your life are you pressing on and growing through perseverance? Talk to Jesus about your needs on this journey.

Grace and peace,
Your fellow pilgrim,
Liena

The Second Week of Lent

Your Way, Your Truth, and Your Life

Dear Reader,

There is nothing like hindsight to make things clear. But very often, when we are right in the middle of events, nothing is clear and nothing is straightforward. It can be very difficult to make sense of what is going on. Jesus' disciple, Thomas, struggles with this uneasy place when he hears Jesus say He is going away while at the same time He says He is the way, the truth, and the life. Let's join Thomas in his struggle and see what the Lord wants to teach us.

Preparing to Reflect

How good it is to center down!
To sit quietly and see one's self pass by!
The streets of our minds seethe with endless traffic;
Our spirits resound with clashing, with noisy silences,
While something deep within hungers and thirsts for the still moment and the resting lull . . .
We look at ourselves in this waiting moment—the kinds of people we are.
The questions persist: what are we doing with our lives?-
what kinds of people we are.
The questions persist: what are we doing with our lives?-
what are the motives that order our days?
What is the end of our doings? Where are we trying to go?
Where do we put the emphases and where are our values focused?
For what end do we make sacrifices?

Where is my treasure and what do I love most in life?

What do I hate most in life and to what am I true?

Over and over the questions beat in upon the waiting moment.

As we listen, floating up through all the jangling echoes of our turbulence, there is a sound of another kind—

A deeper note which only the stillness of the heart makes clear.

It moves directly to the core of our being. Our questions are answered,

Our spirits refreshed, and we move back into the traffic of our daily round

With the peace of the Eternal in our step.

How good it is to center down!

Howard Thurman[1]

I take a moment to step out of my life's noise "traffic," center down, and let God's voice surface above the still waters of my heart.

Prayer

My heart is not proud, LORD,
　　my eyes are not haughty;
I do not concern myself with great matters
　　or things too wonderful for me.
　But I have calmed and quieted myself,
　　I am like a weaned child with its mother;
　　like a weaned child I am content.

Psalm 131:2

Story of the Day

"Do not let your hearts be troubled. You believe in God; believe also in me. My Father's house has many rooms; if that were not so, would I have told you that I am going there to prepare a place for you? And if I go and prepare a place for you, I will come back and take you to be with me that you also may be where I am. You know the way to the place where I am going."

Thomas said to him, "Lord, we don't know where you are going, so how can we know the way?"

Jesus answered, "I am the way and the truth and the life. No one comes to the Father except through me. If you really know me, you will know my Father as well. From now on, you do know him and have seen him" (John 14:1-7).

Entering the Scene

Thomas, puzzled and confused, interrupts Jesus. "Lord, we don't know where You are going. How can we know the way?" Thomas doesn't get it; he doesn't understand what Jesus is telling His followers.

Jesus comes back with a reply, "I am the way, the truth, and the life."

This explanation does not help pragmatic Thomas. Thomas has no idea where Jesus is planning to go, so how can he possibly know the way? *Where* is Jesus going now—and *when*?

Imagine being Thomas for a while and feel his frustration. Can you recall conversations with God when you have asked, "What do You want me to do?"

Jesus answers, "Follow Me."

"Okay, Lord, but what exactly do You want me to *do*?"

Jesus replies again, "Just follow Me."

"There is nothing wrong with Thomas' intelligence. He knew as well as anyone what a way, road, meant. But there was something lacking in his imagination. Literalist as he is, he has a hard time with metaphor. Jesus is using the term *way* or *road* not for something to walk on but as a way of life, a way of doing or saying or praying. But "I am the way"? Jesus is covered with skin, not asphalt. Thomas scratches his head: "'I am the way'? What is he talking about?"[2] Wouldn't you?

Going Deeper

Like Thomas "eventually we catch on: a metaphor both is and is not what is says. And what it doesn't say is more important than what it does say. A metaphor does something that the precision of a definition or an explanation doesn't do: it insists we join the speaker and participate in the creation of a fresh meaning. Metaphor activates our imagination. We begin making connections, joining what we see to something that we don't see right before us, connecting the visible to the invisible. There is more to everything that we can see or hear or touch or taste."[3]

What kind of picture does your imagination paint when you hear Jesus saying, "I am your way, truth, and life"? Take a minute to enjoy the mental landscape of these words.

Jesus comes to open up this invisible world to us. This is why Jesus describes Himself as being "the way" to the Father. In humility and service Jesus "lays down" for us to be "the way" we walk upon. *To follow Jesus is to love the journey with Him.* Journey is an ongoing revelation of the road itself and where it takes us. The only roadmap we have is the truthful person of Jesus and His teachings.

A literal journey, even more a faith journey, cannot be known in an instant; it's a discovery on the go. Some things just can't be rushed. We all have questions we ask God, and we would love to get the answers *now*. If you could talk to God face-to-face today, what would you like to ask Him?

Nevertheless, like Thomas, we need to learn patience. "Be patient toward all that is unsolved in your heart and try to love the questions themselves, like locked rooms and like books that are now written in a very foreign tongue. Do not now seek the answers, which cannot be given you because you would not be able to live them. And the point is, to live everything. Live the questions now. Perhaps you will then gradually, without noticing it, live along some distant day into the answer."[4]

Thomas lives into his answers when he meets the resurrected Jesus and slides his hand into Jesus' wounds. Only then the meaning of way, truth, and life starts unfolding in Thomas' heart and he exclaims, "My Lord and my God!" (John 20:28). Indeed, Jesus is the way into an abundant life that we cannot now even begin to imagine.

Impressions of Jesus' Heart for Your Journey

My child, place your hand into My hand and walk in Me and with Me.

Trust My desire for your highest good. "I have come that they may have life, and have it to the full" (John 10:10).

Your Response

What is your response to Jesus' desire to be your way, truth, and life? Write a short letter to Jesus.

Enjoy the journey,
Your sister in Christ,
Liena

Lasting Peace

God's Beloved,

On the night Jesus was born a company of angels appeared to shepherds watching their flock. They announced the birth of our Savior and proclaimed: "Glory to God in the highest heaven, and on earth peace to those on whom his favor rests" (Luke 2:14). Jesus brings the most precious gift in this world: *peace of heart t*hat comes from a right relationship with the Trinity.

The word we translate as *peace* comes from the Hebrew word shalom, meaning "wholeness," "finished," "complete", and "perfect." *Shalom* describes the deep satisfaction, contentment, and purpose that comes when our hearts beat with the heart of God. Is that something you desire?

Preparing to Reflect

In the stillness of the space that surrounds me, I briefly close my eyes and relax my body. In faith I turn my eyes to the Lord. His gaze is gentle, warm, and overflowing with great affection for me. I capture His expression of love and desire to welcome me into His peace.

I remember David who at the birth of his son, Solomon, pleaded the following prayer, "Grant to Solomon my son a heart of peace" (1 Chronicles 29:19 LEB). In other words, "Let it be in harmony with Your heart, O God. Give him a shalom heart." Is that something I desire to pray for myself as I start today's reflection?

Prayer

Heavenly Father, give me a shalom heart. In the name of Jesus, my Prince of Peace. Amen.

Story of the Day

"Peace I leave with you; my peace I give you. I do not give to you as the world gives. Do not let your hearts be troubled and do not be afraid" (John 14:27).

Entering the Scene

Jesus has told His followers many hard and new things about what is to come after His departure. Imagine being one of the twelve. Wouldn't you feel a little overwhelmed by now? Jesus, knowing His friends' hearts, offers comfort. "Peace I leave with you."

Our Lord's words echo a familiar blessing among the Jews. "Shalom. May you prosper in body and soul, and enjoy every earthy and heavenly good."[5] Yet Jesus does not stop here.

Our Savior uses this common benediction as a foundation for His profound inheritance. Jesus promises *His* peace. Peace that is part of His personhood. It is the same peace He Himself enjoys and draws comfort from in the face of upcoming torture. Our Lord promises to His friends, including you, the contentment that the inhabitants of heaven enjoy.

"When Christ left the world, He made His will. His soul He bequeathed to His Father, and his body to Joseph. His clothes to the soldiers, His mother He left to the care of John. But what should He leave to His poor disciples, who had left all for Him? Silver and gold He had none; but He left them what was far better—His peace."[6]

Going Deeper

When Jesus promises to give us His peace, He means more than a calming emotional state. Our Lord assures the indwelling of an actual person, the Holy Spirit. He is the everlasting Fountain of heaven's shalom. Recall when Jesus appeared to His disciples after the resurrection. He walked through a bolted door to declare: "'Peace be with you! As the Father has sent me, I am sending you.' And with that he breathed on them and said, 'Receive the Holy Spirit'" (John 20:21-22).

The world may wish us peace, but it can never give it to us.

Reflect for a minute on your experience of peace. What is your practice of returning to inner shalom when you get rattled? How do you guard your peace?

I have noticed that I experience internal peace to the degree I embrace, trust, and rest in God's unconditional love for me. Because His love is unconditional, it does not come and go; it underlies everything—both favorable and unfavorable circumstances. "It has something to do with presence—not a future good outcome, but the immediate experience of being met, held in communion, by something intimately at hand."[7]

One of my dear patients is a witness to this beautiful reality. Her response to being diagnosed with cancer has been, "I am not afraid to live, and I am not afraid to die. I do not have peace because He says I will live, I have peace because I have Him who is the Prince of Peace."

Learning to have a heart of peace is a matter of accessing our Prince of Peace who indwells us through His Spirit. God designed us like Jerusalem's temple. The temple's outer court represents our body, its inner court our soul, the holy place our spirit, and the holy of the holies the Holy Spirit's seat in our spirit. At any given time, we can retreat and descend into our holy of the holies to draw peace from the Prince of Peace.

President Truman was asked how he managed to be so calm under the stress of the last days of World War II. "He explained that just as a soldier retreats into his foxhole for protection and rest, so he periodically retired into his own 'mental foxhole' where he allowed nothing to disturb him."[8]

We have the choice of practicing anxiety or practicing the presence of the Prince of Peace in our lives.

Impressions of Jesus' Heart for Your Journey

I am the Creator, the Giver, and the Keeper of your peace. When anxiety intimidates you, start thanking Me for My presence with you. Over and over again say, "Jesus, thank You for being with me." Rest in the assurance that I have you, I hold you, and I carry you.

"Do not be anxious about anything, but in every situation, by prayer and petition, with thanksgiving, present your requests to God" (Philippians 4:6).

Your Response

How are you moved to practice peace in your life? Talk to Jesus about it or express your thoughts to Him in writing.

Guard His peace,
Liena

The Joy of the Lord— Your Shield!

Hello again,

Have you ever struggled to find and keep joy? In today's reflection we will witness Jesus' joy even in the shadow of the cross. His joy is born from above, self-sufficient, and beyond any circumstances.

If you desire to have His joy, come and let Jesus show you the way.

Preparing to Reflect

"Joy is who God is; where He lives from, and what He does. He lives in perpetual everlasting and eternal joy. In His Presence there is fullness of joy. The Father does not give us joy. He gives us Himself. The atmosphere surrounding God is always joyful. We center ourselves in His joy. We breathe it in. We smile because we live under His smile."[9]

As I prepare to pray, I imagine myself approaching God's throne. Pure heavenly joy swirls around me, and rivers of delight flow from my Father's countenance. "Splendor and majesty are before him; strength and joy are in his dwelling place" (1 Chronicles 16:27). I hear the music of laughter. I move forward and lock eyes with my heavenly Father. His face broadens into a smile as He stretches out His hands and welcomes me to pray.

Prayer

My loving God, I thank You that You are joy and delight. "Better is one day in your courts than a thousand elsewhere" (Psalm 84:10). Center me in Your presence so that Your joy would saturate my heart. Amen.

Story of the Day

After Jesus said this, he looked toward heaven and prayed: "Father, the hour has come. Glorify your Son, that your Son may glorify you.

"I am coming to you now, but I say these things while I am still in this world, so that they may have the full measure of my joy within them" (John 17:1, 13).

Entering the Scene

We will spend the next three days with Jesus' prayer in John 17. This is His longest prayer in any of the gospels. It is known as the Farewell Prayer or the High Priest's Prayer. In this prayer Jesus prays for Himself, for His disciples, and for us—His future followers.

The weight of the cross will soon bend Him over, but for now Jesus stands tall with His hands stretched out as if reaching for His Father's face. Jesus is "homesick" for His Father's glory, the glory He left when He "emptied himself" (Philippians 2:7 ESV) and became a man for our sake. Our Lord turns His gaze upward and prayer surges out of His heart.

Imagine standing next to Jesus. What do you see? What is Jesus like when He prays?

Have you ever witnessed someone's prayer being not only a petition, but a revelation of God's heart toward you? This is how Jesus prays.

Going Deeper

Jesus prays aloud not because He is anxious or fearful, but because He wants to assure His followers of the abundance awaiting them. Jesus wants His disciples to see that the kingdom life is *full* of intimacy and glorious riches. There is only one reason He is praying for them, for you, and for me. Jesus' desire is our *complete* joy! Jesus wants His joy to overflow within us. He echoes Nehemiah's words, "Don't be dejected and sad, for the joy of the LORD is your strength!" (Nehemiah 8:10 NLT).

Have you ever reflected on the joy of the Lord, the actual joy experienced in the life of the Trinity? Nothing alters the delight that God feels—the Father for the Son, the Son for the Father, the Holy Spirit dancing between them. Joy and peace sways at the heart of the Trinity. The Scriptures say that this joy is our true strength. Jesus withstands the shock of approaching suffering and death by the power of *His relational joy*. His heart is shielded in joy. What is the essence of His joy?

~ Jesus is joyous because He can look back at His life and say to His Father, "I have brought you glory on earth by finishing the work you gave me to do" (John 17:4). What are the specific ways you enjoy bringing glory to your Father?

~ Jesus' joy stems from deep communion with the Father and the Holy Spirit. Jesus describes His relationship with the Father in the following words, "you are in me and I am in you" (John 17:21). "All I have is yours, and all you have is mine" (John 17:10). How would it feel saying these words in your prayer to the Father?

~ Christ's gladness is the joy of recognized, embraced, and returned love. He says with the utter confidence, "you loved me before the creation of the world" (John 17:24). Do you trust that the Father loves you as much as He loves Jesus?

~ Jesus is overjoyed with expectation of the Father's love for the believers and His own union with them. "I have made you known to them, and will continue to make you known in order that the love you have for me may be in them and that I myself may be in them" (John 17:26). Place your name in this passage and hear Jesus talking to His Father about you in this manner.

~ Jesus' joy lies in anticipation of His coming glory. "And now, Father, glorify me in your presence with the glory I had with you before the world began" (John 17:5). Do you anticipate your glory with Christ?

Our joy lies in pursuing Jesus' joy. "May the God of hope fill you with all joy and peace as you trust in him, so that you may overflow with hope by the power of the Holy Spirit" (Romans 13:15).

Impressions of Jesus' Heart for Your Journey

My beloved, My joy is loving you. "For the LORD your God is living among you. He is a mighty savior. He will take delight in you with gladness. With his love, he will calm all your fears. He will rejoice over you with joyful songs" (Zephaniah 3:17 NLT).

Your Response

Spend some time praying for Jesus' joy to be made complete in you.

May the presence of the Lord enfold you,
Your fellow pilgrim,
Liena

What is Jesus Praying for You?

Dear Pilgrim,

Does prayer ever seem a lonely experience for you? Do you at times struggle with the uncertainty of being heard?

Today's passage assures us that we are not praying alone. Jesus intercedes for us. He prayed for you over two thousand years ago and is still praying for you today.

What has He prayed for you in the past, and what is He praying for you now? Come and be curious about His petition for you.

Preparing to Reflect

Jesus needed solitude to give His full and undivided attention to the Father. To follow His example, I listen for a moment to my favorite music, the sounds in nature, or silence to help me to clear internal space for my communion with God.

I cannot manipulate the experience of grace or prayer, but I can remain sensitive and alert. Once I feel relaxed and focused, I ask the Holy Spirit to accompany me in this time of prayer.

Prayer

Precious Lord, above all things give me a true sensitivity to Your heart's desires. Attune me to the indwelling Holy Spirit to pray according to Your will. Amen.

Story of the Day

"I am not praying for the world, but for those you have given me, for they are yours. All I have is yours, and all you have is mine. And glory

has come to me through them. I will remain in the world no longer, but they are still in the world, and I am coming to you. Holy Father, protect them by the power of your name, the name you gave me, so that they may be one as we are one. While I was with them, I protected them and kept them safe by that name you gave me. None has been lost except the one doomed to destruction so that Scripture would be fulfilled.

"My prayer is not that you take them out of the world but that you protect them from the evil one. They are not of the world, even as I am not of it. Sanctify them by the truth; your word is truth. As you sent me into the world, I have sent them into the world. For them I sanctify myself, that they too may be truly sanctified" (John 17:9-12, 15-19).

Entering the Scene

In His prayer, Jesus clearly finds Himself on the cusp of leaving this world and returning to His glory. Jesus is now in the "home stretch." He stands in the very "thin space" between this world and His Father's kingdom. The visible and invisible merge into intangible oneness. As He prays, the presence of heaven is almost palpable.

I have seen this many times in my work as a chaplain. I watch people move into the space of transcendence when they are dying. Often, my patients' faces light up with blissful smiles, and every so often they stretch out their hands while perceiving heaven's realities through "the thin veil" that separates both worlds.

Watch with me as Jesus parts this thin veil for us in His prayer.

"This chapter has been called the Holy of Holies of Scripture. . . . Here, we are ushered into the throne room of God. Here, we eavesdrop on the communion, the eternal communion between the Son and the Father. The veil is drawn back. We're admitted into the Holy of Holies. We approach the inner communion of the Trinity. The secret place of the Most High God is opened for us. Here, we need to remove our shoes and listen, and humble ourselves with reverent hearts because we are on the holiest of all ground."[10]

Jesus, our High Priest, intercedes for us while standing on this edge, the brink of His coming glory. He gives us a preview of His new ministry which is intercession for us till we come into His glory. "This prayer belongs to us as a gift from heaven so that we know the content of our great High Priest's intercession for us. This is what Jesus is doing now."[11] This is the prayer Jesus has continued to pray for all His followers throughout all ages. Hebrews 7:25 tells us that Jesus always lives to intercede for us. What does this mean to you?

Going Deeper

When people are close to dying, they say the most necessary and important things. What does Jesus find to be absolutely essential in His prayer for His disciples?

Through His obedience Jesus has earned an inheritance for His disciples, including us. Now He prays that the Father would distribute and activate this legacy in His followers' lives.

What is our inheritance from Jesus? It is His words to purify us, His name to protect us, His ministry to continue, His truth to discern well, and His love to unite us. Jesus prays that His followers will reflect the same quality of intimacy that the Father, Son, and the Holy Spirit enjoy. Do you frequently join Jesus in praying for the same things?

The Scriptures assure us that Jesus is still interceding for us today. "Who then is the one who condemns? No one. Christ Jesus who died—more than that, who was raised to life—is at the right hand of God and is also interceding for us" (Romans 8:34). What does this mean for our prayer life today? How can we join Jesus in praying for our specific struggles and circumstances?

The indwelling Holy Spirit is the very presence of Christ within us. Paying close attention to Him leads to understanding what Christ is praying for us. True prayer always originates in God and returns to God. "What if prayer is not praying towards God but praying with God? Prayer is about finding out what God wants to do and then asking Him to do it."[12]

"In my experience in churches and friendships, I have seen that when we pray too soon, we usually pray in unbelief. We find ourselves praying out of the shock of trauma of the situation itself, and we pray out of our panic, our worry, our anxiety, and our concern."[13]

Listening before we pray is essential if we want to pray *with* God. A sister in Christ shares her experience of "hammering away" without listening. "Intercession is much better if it is done with a quality of listening and gazing at a situation, and keeping an open alertness about all the ways the Lord might intervene. More than once I have found that my hammering-type intercessory prayer was actually hammering at the wrong place—as if I had been trying to get a door to open by banging away with all my might, then realizing that I was not standing in front of the door at all, but just bruising my knuckles on a stretch of wall."[14]

When I pray for my patients in the hospital, I usually pause in an effort to detect in my spirit what the Holy Spirit is praying for this specific person. At times my encounters look rather humorous. Once before praying for an elderly gentleman, I took his hand in mine and paused. He shouted, "Are you going to pray or not?" I responded with my eyes closed, "I am listening!"

How would your prayer life be different if in every crisis, need, or dilemma you stilled yourself before the Lord and asked the following questions: Lord, help me to perceive how You are moving in this situation and to pray accordingly. Change me according to Your desired outcome for this situation. Lord Holy Spirit, give me impressions of how to pray.

Listening to the indwelling Holy Spirit and His voice in the Scriptures puts us on the path of our prayers always being answered.

Impressions of Jesus' Heart for Your Journey

I bid you, My child, to the fellowship of prayer. I intercede for you, and when you don't know how to pray, the Holy Spirit intercedes for you as well. Incline your heart to Our prayer.

"The Spirit helps us in our weakness. We do not know what we ought to pray for, but the Spirit himself intercedes for us through wordless groans" (Romans 8:26).

Your Response

What is stirred up in you right now? What challenges you? What comforts you? Express your heart to God in journaling and prayer.

Your friend in prayer,
Liena

Dance with the Trinity

Dear Friend,

Do you ever wonder about the relationship in the heart of the Holy Trinity? What does this inner relationship of love look like? And how is this relationship relevant to your own life?

Jesus gains for us a reestablished entry into the inner fellowship of God's life. In His farewell prayer, Jesus petitions for us to take full advantage of this offer. Come and explore with me how you can live the answer to Jesus' prayer.

Preparing to Reflect

It is a privilege to come before the throne of the living God. Before I pray, I take a moment to appreciate this gift of being always welcomed and heard. I still and attune myself to God's presence with me.

I envision the circle of the Holy Trinity motioning me to become part of this circle. I imagine myself stepping into this circle and greeting each member of the Trinity. What do I say?

Prayer

Thank You, Father, Son, and Holy Spirit for welcoming me into the circle of Your love. Thank You for Your desire to reveal the beauty of Your relationship to me and through me to others. Amen.

Story of the Day

"My prayer is not for them alone. I pray also for those who will believe in me through their message, that all of them may be one, Father, just as you are in me and I am in you. May they also be in us so that the world

may believe that you have sent me. I have given them the glory that you gave me, that they may be one as we are one— I in them and you in me—so that they may be brought to complete unity. Then the world will know that you sent me and have loved them even as you have loved me.

"Father, I want those you have given me to be with me where I am, and to see my glory, the glory you have given me because you loved me before the creation of the world.

"Righteous Father, though the world does not know you, I know you, and they know that you have sent me. I have made you known to them, and will continue to make you known in order that the love you have for me may be in them and that I myself may be in them" (John 17:20-26).

Entering the Scene

Feel the *passion* of Jesus prayer! Hear *the depth* of His words! Jesus prays for what is His highest priority and deepest desire: complete union with His followers and unity among His disciples. There is nothing more important to Him than Christians being committed to overcoming contentions and being devoted to loving each other. Why is that so important to Him? Because it's the only real witness of the utmost unity within the life of the Trinity. It's the sole way of reflecting "the love dance" of the Father, the Son, and the Holy Spirit.

God is not some faceless, all-powerful abstraction. God is the Father, Son and Spirit, existing in a passionate and joyous fellowship. The Trinity is not three highly committed religious types sitting around some room in heaven. The Trinity is a circle of shared life, and the life shared is full, not empty, abounding and rich and beautiful, not lonely and sad and boring. The river begins right there, in the fellowship of the Trinity. The great dance is all about the abounding *life* shared by the Father, Son and Spirit. The incarnation is the staggering act of this God reaching out to share their great dance with us. Our humanity is the theater in and through which the great dance is played out in our lives, and human history is the harrowing experience through which we are educated as to the truth of our identity.

There is only one circle of life in the universe, and we belong to it. . . . We belong to the Father, the Son and the Holy Spirit.[15]

C. B. Kruger indicates that everything you enjoy and treasure most in this life—the beauty of parenthood, play, and the pleasure of love—are all the Great Dance playing out through the senses of your life.[16]

What do you treasure the most? Do you feel part of this Divine Dance? Imagine Jesus extending His hand to pull you into the Dance. Will you take it? Will you be the answer to His prayer?

Going Deeper

God invites you to dwell in the circle of His inner relationship of love. Do you believe it? What happens when you accept this invitation? Into what are you drawn? Let's look for a moment at the dynamics of this relationship at the center of the universe.

A waterwheel is a beautiful symbol for the life of Trinity. Visualize the water flowing from paddle to paddle as the wheel turns around. It's an illustration of how the Father, the Son, and the Holy Spirit pour themselves into each other and for the other. All members of the Trinity continually serve and support one another. The Father's joy is to love the Son. "This is my dearly loved Son, who brings me great joy" (Matthew 3:17 NLT). The Son's delight is to serve the Father: "'My food,' said Jesus, 'is to do the will of him who sent me and to finish his work'" (John 4:34). And the Spirit's honor is to give witness to Jesus. "When the Helper comes, whom I will send to you from the Father, that is the Spirit of truth who proceeds from the Father, He will testify about Me" (John 15:26 NASB). The Trinity constantly supports each other in what they are doing in heaven and on this earth.

God's presence in this world is the overflow of the Trinitarian relationship. "The waterwheel" spills over because it's not capable of containing itself. Love has to flow!

Have you experienced that in your relationships? When you are in love or loved by another human being or God, you want to embrace the entire world. You want to share, you want to give and to create life together. In our own desires we see God's image and likeness. Behold the beauty of the Lord in your own soul!

To live a holy life is to be connected to God and allow the Trinity to stream through us. To sin is to be disconnected from the Trinitarian life and to stop this Great Flow in our daily living.

Reflect on moments when you were aware of being part of this Great Flow in your relationships. What was it like? And now reflect on instances when you stopped it. What did you experience? Examine your life through Jesus' words, "For the Scriptures declare that rivers of living water shall flow from the inmost being of anyone who believes in me" (John 7:38 TLB).

Impressions of Jesus' Heart for your Journey

Dear One, join Us in this dance. Take Our hand and let Us guide you step by step in time to the music of the abundant life that We desire for you. Open your heart, mind, and spirit to allow the unobstructed flow of Our grace and mercy.

Your Response

Does today's reflection inspire you to live your life differently? Journal your specific intentions and pray for them.

Join the Great Dance,
Liena

Come Out!

Christ's Beloved,

Jesus is on the doorstep of His own death and resurrection when the Father lets Him be part of Lazarus' resurrection. Lazarus foreshadows Jesus' journey and becomes a source of great encouragement for Him.

How has someone else's emotional, spiritual, or physical healing inspired you to shed off your own "graveclothes" and embrace the life that Jesus offers? Or do you still feel wrapped in "bandages" of a particular struggle, addiction, or negative feelings? Come with me to the grave of Lazarus and let Jesus perform a miracle in your life.

Preparing to Reflect

As I come to my special meeting place with God, I turn my thoughts to Him, leaving aside my chores and preoccupations.

I center down and, for a moment, picture God's actual goodness pursuing me as described in the twenty-third psalm. "Only goodness and faithful love will pursue me all the days of my life, and I will dwell in the house of the LORD as long as I live" (Psalm 23:6 CSB).

Prayer

Lord, I thank You for Your faithful pursuit of me. Amen.

Story of the Day

Do you remember Mary, who poured the costly perfume on Jesus' feet and wiped them with her hair? Well, her brother Lazarus, who lived in Bethany with Mary and her sister Martha, was sick. So the two sisters sent a message to Jesus telling him, "Sir, your good friend is very, very sick."

But when Jesus heard about it he said, "The purpose of his illness is not death, but for the glory of God. I, the Son of God, will receive glory from this situation."

Although Jesus was very fond of Martha, Mary, and Lazarus, he stayed where he was for the next two days and made no move to go to them. Finally, after the two days, he said to his disciples, "Let's go to Judea."

When they arrived at Bethany, they were told that Lazarus had already been in his tomb for four days. Bethany was only a couple of miles down the road from Jerusalem, and many of the Jewish leaders had come to pay their respects and to console Martha and Mary on their loss. When Martha got word that Jesus was coming, she went to meet him. But Mary stayed at home.

Martha said to Jesus, "Sir, if you had been here, my brother wouldn't have died. And even now it's not too late, for I know that God will bring my brother back to life again, if you will only ask him to."

Jesus told her, "Your brother will come back to life again."

"Yes," Martha said, "when everyone else does, on Resurrection Day."

Jesus told her, "I am the one who raises the dead and gives them life again. Anyone who believes in me, even though he dies like anyone else, shall live again. He is given eternal life for believing in me and shall never perish. Do you believe this, Martha?"

"Yes, Master," she told him. "I believe you are the Messiah, the Son of God, the one we have so long awaited."

Then she left him and returned to Mary and, calling her aside from the mourners, told her, "He is here and wants to see you." So Mary went to him at once.

Now Jesus had stayed outside the village, at the place where Martha met him. When the Jewish leaders who were at the house trying to console Mary saw her leave so hastily, they assumed she was going to Lazarus' tomb to weep; so they followed her.

When Mary arrived where Jesus was, she fell down at his feet, saying, "Sir, if you had been here, my brother would still be alive."

When Jesus saw her weeping and the Jewish leaders wailing with her, he was moved with indignation and deeply troubled. "Where is he buried?" he asked them.

They told him, "Come and see." Tears came to Jesus' eyes.

"They were close friends," the Jewish leaders said. "See how much he loved him."

But some said, "This fellow healed a blind man—why couldn't he keep Lazarus from dying?"

And again Jesus was moved with deep anger. Then they came to the tomb. It was a cave with a heavy stone rolled across its door.

"Roll the stone aside," Jesus told them.

But Martha, the dead man's sister, said, "By now the smell will be terrible, for he has been dead four days."

"But didn't I tell you that you will see a wonderful miracle from God if you believe?" Jesus asked her.

So they rolled the stone aside. Then Jesus looked up to heaven and said, "Father, thank you for hearing me. (You always hear me, of course, but I said it because of all these people standing here, so that they will believe you sent me.)" Then he shouted, "Lazarus, come out!"

And Lazarus came—bound up in the grave cloth, his face muffled in a head swath. Jesus told them, "Unwrap him and let him go!" (John 11:1-7, 17-44 TLB).

Entering the Scene

Instead of rushing to Lazarus, Jesus waits in obedience to His Father's timing. Jesus has a different purpose in His mind. "If Jesus had simply healed Lazarus, I'm sure some there would be praising God. I'm also sure some skeptics have claimed he wasn't actually *that* sick. But when someone's been dead for four days, there's pretty much only one explanation. Healing Laz before he died would have definitely reinforced the faith they already had. But Jesus wanted *to stretch* their faith. It's just a fact of life: sometimes things have to go from bad to worse before they get better!"[17]

When Jesus finally arrives, Lazarus' tomb is already sealed. The tomb was accessible for the first couple of days, then sealed as decomposition began. Lazarus' body, wrapped in strips of linen cloth, lies still like a mummy in a stone cave.

Accordingly, Martha is quick to say that Jesus is too late. For Martha and Mary, the prime window of divine opportunity closed when Lazarus drew his last breath.

What feels too late in your life?

Grief and anger spills over in Jesus' heart—grief because of His love for Lazarus and his sisters, and anger because of what death does to them. Burning with passion, Jesus thanks the Father for hearing His prayer, then He steps toward the entrance and shouts, *"Lazarus, come out!"* Everyone at the tomb is surprised at Jesus' daring. Some even think He is out of His mind. The authors of *The Grave Robber*[18] allude that it is an all-or-nothing moment for both Lazarus and Jesus.

When have you dared greatly and held your breath in waiting?

The stakes cannot be any higher, and *that* is how most miracles happen. What if Lazarus hears but chooses not to respond? What if Lazarus feels powerless, too helpless to help himself? What if he turns a deaf ear to His call? When Jesus tells Lazarus to come out, Jesus pushes all His chips to the middle of the table and bets it all.

Lazarus steps out.

For a moment imagine being Lazarus. What is it like to be tossed back from the afterlife into the present reality of the people you left four days ago? Picture yourself, enshrouded with pounds of linen strips, struggling to sit up. You shake your head side to side to loosen the head wrapping to breathe again. Then you expend great effort to rise. Tied up the way you are and still smelling of decay, you shuffle to the entrance of the tomb where Jesus tells the people standing around to hurry up and help you to get free of your graveclothes. How does it feel to see the sunlight again?

When our Lord lays His eyes on Lazarus, He sees His own resurrection only a few days away. And Jesus sees the future of all of us being resurrected before the throne of God.

Imagine now being Jesus. What does this experience mean for you?

Going Deeper

Notice the emotional response Jesus has when He meets Martha and her grieving friends. Jesus does not approach them in a distant, clinical manner. He meets them in their sorrow! Jesus sobs. God does not discount or minimize our pain. Jesus feels every sorrow, every loss, and every death as His own.

And Jesus doesn't just get sad, He gets mad! John confides that Jesus is moved with anger. He is angry at death. Have you been angry at death? God never intended that we suffer from the deterioration set in motion with the fall in Eden.

Death makes Jesus mad enough to take it on the cross and destroy it at the source.

I often have conversations with family members at the hospital who have lost their loved ones. In our sorrow we often displace our anger. We blame God instead of the evil one. I often say, "Remember: *death takes, God receives*." There is a big difference between those two. Because God is so intimately close to us in death and sorrow, we often confuse His presence with Him being a cause of these afflictions. Jesus disarms death through His dying. Even more, He makes death to work *for* us. On the day of Jesus' resurrection, "Death itself would start working backwards."[19] Death becomes a birth channel into eternal life. Can you imagine how shocked, debilitated, and surprised the Devil was on Easter morning?

In the story of Lazarus we see how three components come together for the healing miracle to take place: Jesus' intervention, Lazarus' effort, and the help of his community.

Notice how Jesus tells the people around Lazarus to free him from the graveclothes. How have you experienced all these healing blocks working together in your journey? One thing is for certain: healing requires persevering cooperation. What does your next right step look like?

When Jesus says to Lazarus *"Come out,"* how can you apply these words to your life? I've heard the command of Jesus to come out! Have you?

~ Come out of that angry place!

~ Shake off your bitterness!

~ Let go of your hurt!

~ Throw off the excuses; shake out of your discouragement!

What is Jesus calling you to come out of *right now*?

Impressions of Jesus' Heart for Your Journey

Come out, My child! Have courage and respond to Me. I am your resurrection and life even now. Throw off your rotting graveclothes, put on the fresh linens of My giving. "Have I not commanded you? Be strong and courageous. Do not be afraid; do not be discouraged, for the LORD your God will be with you wherever you go" (Joshua 1:9).

Your Response

What is your response to Jesus' words, "Come out!"? Talk to the Lord and write to Him.

In prayer for your freedom,
Liena

_____
_____
_____
_____
_____
_____
_____
_____
_____
_____
_____
_____
_____
_____
_____
_____
_____
_____
_____
_____
_____
_____
_____
_____

Love Poured Out

Greetings,

Have you been surprised by the caring sensitivity of someone just at the moment you felt overwhelmed by grief or uncertainty? A gift was given, a meal was shared, a note was sent, and you received the kindness of a listening ear.

We sometimes think that God is above all this, that He cannot possibly know what it is to feel lonely or lost or afraid. But in today's story we witness the gratitude Jesus expresses when Mary, Lazarus' sister, takes the time to understand His sorrow and responds. What is the invitation for you in today's story?

Preparing to Reflect

Prayer has many facets like any relationship. One of them is ministering to our Lord in love or consoling His heart. This prayer is lived out in our daily life through comforting Christ in others who suffer.

I settle down in my prayer chair, quiet down, and meditate for a few minutes on this aspect of prayer.

Prayer

Lord,
give us faith
to know You
in Your direct need . . .
In those who do not look like You.
who do not speak like You,
who perhaps do not even know You
though You are suffering in them.[20]

Story of the Day

Meanwhile, the leading priests and Pharisees had publicly ordered that anyone seeing Jesus must report it immediately so they could arrest Him.

Six days before the Passover celebration began, Jesus arrived in Bethany, the home of Lazarus—the man he had raised from the dead. A dinner was prepared in Jesus' honor. Martha served, and Lazarus was among those who ate with Him. Then Mary took a twelve-ounce jar of expensive perfume made from essence of nard, and she anointed Jesus' feet with it, wiping His feet with her hair. The house was filled with the fragrance.

But Judas Iscariot, the disciple who would soon betray Him, said, "That perfume was worth a year's wages. It should have been sold and the money given to the poor." Not that he cared for the poor—he was a thief, and since he was in charge of the disciples' money, he often stole some for himself.

Jesus replied, "Leave her alone. She did this in preparation for my burial. You will always have the poor among you, but you will not always have me."

When all the people heard of Jesus' arrival, they flocked to see Him and also to see Lazarus, the man Jesus had raised from the dead. Then the leading priests decided to kill Lazarus, too, for it was because of him that many of the people had deserted them and believed in Jesus (John 11:57—12:11 NLT).

Entering the Scene

By now the shadow of the cross accompanies Jesus wherever He goes; the days before His crucifixion are numbered—six, to be precise. The accusers are after Jesus, and impending denial and death taunts Him at every turn. Where can He go for understanding and comfort? His heart longs for a family circle that will surround Him on His deathbed and reassure Him with their love.

The Father is mindful of His Son's needs and directs Jesus again to the home of Lazarus, Martha, and Mary—this time with a different purpose. A fine dinner is prepared in Jesus' honor and in celebration of Lazarus' resurrection. The savory aroma fills the dwelling.

Finally, the meal is ready, and the guests take their places around the table. They are filled with their own thoughts and priorities, and the conversation reflects this preoccupation. Imagine that you are one of them. What do you notice about the other guests? What is the atmosphere in the room?

Jesus is silent as the conversation swirls around Him. He looks from one face to the other. When His eyes come to rest on yours, what does He see? What do you feel? Take a moment to reflect on this.

Jesus moves His gaze to rest on Lazarus—the living and foreshadowing icon of Jesus' own resurrection. What do you think Jesus feels as He watches Lazarus laughing with the man seated next to him? If you were Jesus, aware of what is coming in the next few days, what strength might you draw from the presence of Lazarus?

The conversation around the table quiets as the guests enjoy the delicious meal. Suddenly Mary enters the room. Her eyes are fixed on Jesus, and she carries with her an alabaster bottle of very expensive perfume. Ignoring the startled glances exchanged around the table, Mary drops to her knees in front of Jesus. Imagine yourself being Mary. What internal force is pulling you toward Jesus? What instinct drives you to ignore social convention to do what you are about to do?

Mary breaks open the top of the bottle with a swift motion. The fragrance fills the room, overwhelming all other smells with its rich scent. The guests watch, stunned, as Mary pours the entire bottle over the feet of Jesus. He does not pull back; Jesus opens Himself fully to receive Mary's tender expression of love. As the oil seeps into the cells of His being, so does the compassion, comfort, and love that fills Mary's heart. She herself is the offering poured out for Him. Wrapping her hair around His feet like a towel, Mary ministers to Jesus' troubled heart and prepares Him for His burial.

"Do we hesitate to believe what this text suggests—that the effusive affection of Mary not only prepared the body of Jesus but meant something to the heart of Jesus that only he might have guessed and prepared and sustained His soul as he faced all that led to his burial."[21] Jesus recognizes her intention and receives her gift with profound gratitude. He will never forget her kindness. It will be memorialized forever.

Going Deeper

The story compels a further question: Does Mary fully know what she is doing? Does she realize the prophetic significance of her actions? Most likely not. She intuits Jesus' need through love. "God can only be known by loving God. The mystics would say whenever you stand apart and objectify anything, you stop knowing it. You have to love, respect, and enter into relationship with what you desire to know. Then the loving becomes its own kind of knowing. This is knowing by participation."[22] Mary's sacrificial path of loving Jesus fully distinguishes her from the other guests.

How has loving Jesus led you into a deeper understanding of His heart?

Only deep and self-forgetting love unleashes us to complete freedom. In the presence of Jesus, the world and its opinions fade away. Had this not been so, Mary never would have had the freedom to do for Jesus what He so desperately needed done. Her love for Him pulled Mary through layers of logic, customs, rules, and opinions to discover a pure union with Him.

Have you had the experience in worship where the Holy Spirit takes possession of your heart in adoration and praise? The world around you disappears. You give no thought to whether you sit, stand, dance, kneel, or weep. You are free to be present with Jesus as was Mary.

Mary of Bethany may be found at the feet of Jesus in every one of the four Gospels. The posture of bold humility is the core of her being. In Luke 10:39 Mary sits at Jesus' feet and listens attentively to all that is on His mind. She refuses to be dissuaded, even when her frustrated sister demands that she help prepare the meal. In John 11:32 Mary falls at His feet lamenting that had Jesus come sooner, her brother Lazarus would not have died. Yet Mary trusts Jesus for what He will do even now. "Humility has absolute power over God's heart, and attracts the fullness of His grace."[23]

What if the key to answered prayer is not more prayer, but rather a focus on what is of primary importance to Jesus? "Delight yourself in the LORD, and he will give you the desires of your heart" (Psalm 37:4 ESV).What if it is our humility and love that moves Jesus to act the most? How could this change the way we pray?

Impressions of Jesus' Heart for Your Journey

Oh, My beloved, nothing touches Me more deeply than your humility, and nothing soothes My aching heart more than your adoring love. When you fall on your knees before Me, I rise up to act on your behalf. You are undefeatable when your face rests on My feet.

Your Response

How does Mary's disposition to live at the feet of Jesus move you? What desire rises within you? Write your love letter to the Lord.

Grace and peace,
Your friend, Liena

The Third Week of Lent

The Servant King

Dear Reader,

We probably all, at some point in our lives, have experienced the effect of the abuse of power resulting in deep emotional wounds and a mistrust of authority. These experiences can make our surrender to God difficult.

Jesus knows our human struggle with submission. After Mary's anointing, Jesus arrives in Jerusalem on a donkey—undercutting any notion of God being an oppressive king. Jesus is deliberate and intentional in His challenge of our traditional perception of power. He comes to serve. Can you trust this kind of king? How can this trust grow?

Preparing to Reflect

I take a few minutes to become still and center myself in God's presence. I imagine Jesus riding toward me on the donkey. What song of praise do I want to sing to Him? I continue by playing or singing a hymn or worship song to my king.

Prayer

Lord Jesus Christ, whose greatest moments of triumph happen
   on the back of a donkey's foal
    and nailed to a bloody cross,
We gather to prepare the way for You
   in our lives and in our world.

There are so many people and things that call for our allegiance
   so many kings seeking to rule over us.
But, You ride into our experience as another kind of King

a serving, humble and challenging King
  who calls us not to slavery, but friendship.

There are so many things that seek our energy and resources
for their own sakes
  so many Kingdoms seeking our souls for their own glory.
But, You ride into our experience heralding another kind of
Kingdom
  a Kingdom where the least are the greatest,
    where the meek inherit the earth
    and where children are the best example of citizenship.
  a Kingdom which seeks to bring life, not drain it.

There are so many things that draw our attention.
  So many realities that seek our faith and assent.
But, You ride into our experience revealing another kind of reality
  a reality where death does not have the last word.
  a reality where pride, selfishness and evil are defeated
    by love and self-giving.
  a reality which does not parade itself for all to see,
  but fills every moment, every situation and every thing with life,
    while waiting for us to discover it.

And so, we cry, from our hearts
  Hosanna, Save us.
  Blessed is He Who comes in the Name of the Lord.
Amen.

John van de Laar[1]

Story of the Day

As he approached Bethphage and Bethany at the hill called the Mount of Olives, he sent two of his disciples, saying to them, "Go to the village ahead of you, and as you enter it, you will find a colt tied there, which no one has ever ridden. Untie it and bring it here. If anyone asks you, 'Why are you untying it?' say, 'The Lord needs it.'"

Those who were sent ahead went and found it just as he had told them. As they were untying the colt, its owners asked them, "Why are you untying the colt?"

They replied, "The Lord needs it."

They brought it to Jesus, threw their cloaks on the colt and put Jesus on it. As he went along, people spread their cloaks on the road.

When he came near the place where the road goes down the Mount of Olives, the whole crowd of disciples began joyfully to praise God in loud voices for all the miracles they had seen:

"Blessed is the king who comes in the name of the Lord!"

"Peace in heaven and glory in the highest!"

Some of the Pharisees in the crowd said to Jesus, "Teacher, rebuke your disciples!"

"I tell you," he replied, "if they keep quiet, the stones will cry out" (Luke 19:29-40).

Entering the Scene

The people of Jerusalem have seen their share of processions: kings and rulers riding on warhorses and stallions, dressed in protective armor, and accompanied by guards. Golden chariots have clattered and flashed through the streets of Jerusalem. But the people have never seen anything like this—their self-proclaimed king entering the city gate on a donkey! All other rulers have entered on magnificent steeds; this one arrives on a never-ridden colt! The people can feel it in their hearts: something unprecedented is about to take place.

Imagine sitting behind Jesus, swaying back and forth with the movement of the foal's short and jarring steps. The lingering fragrance on Jesus' hair, clothes, and feet remind Him and you of the profuse, generous love expressed by Mary. How do you feel? Embarrassed, awkward, or perhaps elated? How would you describe your ride to your friends?

Jesus leads a large crowd. These are the people who have witnessed His many miracles. The poor and healed lepers leap with joy. All the "nobodies" pave the road before Jesus with their outer garments. The palm branches crush under the feet of the virgin donkey.

"Hosanna!" echoes from one street building to another. Shouts of hope flood the town,

"Blessed is he who comes in the name of the Lord!"

"Blessed is the coming kingdom of our father David!"

"Hosanna in the highest heaven!" (Mark 11:9-10).

Dazed with euphoria the crowd recalls Prince Solomon, the heir of King David, riding on a mule and being anointed as king (1 Kings 1:32-40). Yes, it will happen! Jesus will be the next King. Zachariah's prophecy is fulfilled today,

> Rejoice greatly, Daughter Zion!
> Shout, Daughter Jerusalem!
> See, your king comes to you,
> righteous and victorious,
> lowly and riding on a donkey,
> on a colt, the foal of a donkey.
> Zechariah 9:9-10

Going Deeper

True, willing, and joyful surrender is only possible when we know Jesus to be the Servant king, *empowering us,* and *lifting us up* and *out* of entanglements with falsity, fears, and limitations. Jesus the King does not mandate surrender, *He loves us into the desire to surrender.*

There have been numerous times I have heard from my patients, "I struggle to pray *Thy will be done.* I am afraid something bad will happen," or "I am fearful of imposed limitations." Have you ever felt that way? So, instead of praying with them, *Thy will be done,* I often substitute, "Lord, may Your love, wisdom, and goodness be done" as a way of clarifying for my patient what the will of God is for all of His beloved children. God's will is *always good* and *only good.*

Only in the context of a love relationship with God do we learn to trust Him completely. Any tension between our freedom and God's will resolves naturally. "Nothing but love can resolve the contradiction between two freedoms: only love enables two freedoms to unite freely."[2] In loving God we start experiencing the most beautiful paradox of surrender, leading us into greater freedom.

People who go through life with the Lord and let themselves be led by him experience a growing feeling of freedom. Their hearts are not constrained or stifled, but expand and "breathe" ever more freely. God is infinite love; there is nothing narrow or confined about him. Everything in him is wide and spacious. Those who travel with God feel free; they feel that they have nothing to fear, that they are not subject to control, but on the contrary that everything is subject to them because everything works together for their good, whether favorable or unfavorable circumstances, good or bad. They feel that everything belongs to them, because God belongs to them. They are not subject to conditions but always do what they want because what they want is to love, and that is always within their power. Nothing can separate them from the God they love; and they feel that even if they were in prison, they would be just as happy, because there is no way that any power in the world can take God way from them.[3]

What blessings of surrender to Jesus have you experienced in your life? How is He working in your life now to make you free?

Impressions of Jesus' Heart for Your Journey

My child, pray for grace to love Me more deeply. Love makes surrender to Me enticing, melting away all resistance and fears. "I have come in order that you might have life—life in all its fullness" (John 10:10 GNT).

Your Response

How do you want the Lord to help you give your heart more fully to Him? What holds you back? I invite you to voice or write your prayers.

May you know the joy of surrender,
Your sister in Christ,
Liena

What Has Jesus Done for You?

God's Beloved,

Vulnerability is hard, yet it is *the only way* we can be truly connected to each other and to the Lord. I invite you to come sit with me before Jesus and let Him minister to the very core of who we are.

Preparing to Reflect

"I will praise you as long as I live, and in your name I will lift up my hands" (Psalm 63:4).

Given the close connection between my mind and body, I might choose to stand as I begin my prayer time. I raise my open hands to shoulder height. This is the traditional posture for prayer in Hebraic and also Christian traditions. I take a few slow, deep breaths and extend my heart towards God. I take a moment to praise Him and confess that my heart is ready to receive Him.

Prayer

Lord, I open my heart to You. Surprise me with Your goodness today. Amen.

Story of the Day

It was just before the Passover Festival. Jesus knew that the hour had come for him to leave this world and go to the Father. Having loved his own who were in the world, he loved them to the end.

The evening meal was in progress, and the devil had already prompted

Judas, the son of Simon Iscariot, to betray Jesus. Jesus knew that the Father had put all things under his power, and that he had come from God and was returning to God; so he got up from the meal, took off his outer clothing, and wrapped a towel around his waist. After that, he poured water into a basin and began to wash his disciples' feet, drying them with the towel that was wrapped around him.

He came to Simon Peter, who said to him, "Lord, are you going to wash my feet?"

Jesus replied, "You do not realize now what I am doing, but later you will understand."

"No," said Peter, "you shall never wash my feet."

Jesus answered, "Unless I wash you, you have no part with me."

"Then, Lord," Simon Peter replied, "not just my feet but my hands and my head as well!"

Jesus answered, "Those who have had a bath need only to wash their feet; their whole body is clean. And you are clean, though not every one of you." For he knew who was going to betray him, and that was why he said not everyone was clean.

When he had finished washing their feet, he put on his clothes and returned to his place. "Do you understand what I have done for you?" he asked them. "You call me 'Teacher' and 'Lord,' and rightly so, for that is what I am. Now that I, your Lord and Teacher, have washed your feet, you also should wash one another's feet. I have set you an example that you should do as I have done for you. Very truly I tell you, no servant is greater than his master, nor is a messenger greater than the one who sent him. Now that you know these things, you will be blessed if you do them" (John 13:1-17).

Entering the Scene

Jesus arrives at the Last Supper knowing that He is only steps away from the road to Calvary. Up to this point, our Lord has walked under His Father's unique protection because the hour had not come yet. Now Jesus' life is unshielded and exposed to those who seek to kill Him. He has never been more vulnerable than at this hour.

Jesus could back out anytime. He could stop all this anguish in a heartbeat, yet—He came to this earth to give His life away as a servant. Service would be the last will He writes on His disciples' hearts with the loving strokes of a towel.

Jesus pulls Himself up in the middle of the supper. "What is He up to?" all curiously question. Jesus' steady gaze beholds the inquiring disciples as He carefully lays aside His outer garments and exchanges them for a towel lying neglected next to the wash basin. His shocking gesture conveys an explicit message, "I am laying down My life for you." Jesus' disciples stop eating. An awkward hush pervades the room and halfway broken bread falls back onto the table. Jesus reaches for the water jar and deliberately pours the water in the basin. Do you hear the stream of water in the hallowed silence of the room?

To the amazement of Jesus' disciples, He kneels at their feet. If you were one of "twelve", how would you react? Place yourself honestly and wholeheartedly in the scene.

Going Deeper

Jesus moves from one disciple to the next, recalling the sacred journey they have shared together and simultaneously foreseeing His companions' betrayal in just a few hours. How hard it must be to overcome the human inclination to withdraw in self-protection and to withhold His love. Yet "having loved his own who were in the world, he loved them to the end" (John 13:1). Anything less than perfect love would renounce His being.

This is also true for us who follow the way of Jesus in life. The deepest joy and fulfilment comes with loving someone to the end. The most gut-wrenching sorrow comes from experiencing our limitations and failing this journey. Pause for a moment to ask yourself some questions. Who have I loved to the very end? What was it like? Who has loved me to the very end? How has their love changed and inspired me?

It is very hard to let the Lord's *absolute* love penetrate our being.

We see our collective resistance in Peter, who asked, "Lord, are you going to wash my feet?"

Jesus replies, "You do not realize now what I am doing, but later you will understand.

"No," said Peter, "you shall never wash my feet!" (John 13:6-8).

Jesus looks at Peter with sadness and reveals a striking implication. "Unless I wash you, you have no part with me" (John 13:8).

"Unless you allow Me to touch the darkest, the dirtiest, and the most shameful parts in you, we are complete strangers to each other." The depth of our vulnerability *equates* to the extent of our communion with the Lord. True spiritual transformation is always about consenting to the Lord's humble cleansing. Confession of sin is never enough for one's heart to be changed. It has to pair with allowing Jesus to touch our sin and struggle.

What has your journey of vulnerability with Jesus been like? Do you allow Jesus to touch your shame and pain through the loving care of others?

I will never forget the day when my college friend came to me and said, "Liena, you listen so well to all our sorrows and secrets, but none of us knows your heart." That day marked the beginning of my willingness to be slowly disclosed before others and enter the true communion of souls through *shared vulnerability.*

After washing the disciples' feet, Jesus asks them, "Do you understand what I have done for you?" What *has* He done for them? The disciples are on the brink of entering great confusion, disloyalty, and chaos. Is He forgiving them before they mutter their confessions? Are they cleansed once for all time? Is He saying, "It will be well with your souls as you remember to fall back on My love in the darkest of hours?"

Impressions of Jesus's Heart for Your Journey

My precious child, do you know that My deepest joy comes from your receptivity? As you truly allow Me to touch you, you will be cleansed and healed. Can you trust that I am tender and gentle at heart? I long for you to be with Me without the need to conceal any of your darkness. Be brave enough to let Me love you!

Your Response

What is your response to Jesus' invitation? If you feel moved, use this time to uncover yourself before Him in prayer and writing.

Your sister in Christ,
Liena

Are You a Welcoming Host of the Host?

My Dear Lent Friend,

There is a deep correlation between experiencing God's presence in our lives and providing an internal space for His presence. Any true relationship provides a hunger, an openness, and an eagerness to receive the other. In any trusting relationship the partakers *surrender* to each other and avail themselves to the partner's influence. It is true in our walk with God as well. "It is not enough to be aware of another. It is essential that we be open to him, if the possibilities of our relationship are to become a reality. Until we are open . . . the Presence is immobilized."[4] I invite you to take a fresh look at your hospitality to Jesus as He surrenders Himself joyfully to *you* in the communion elements of wine and bread.

Preparing to Reflect

To help my spirit to pray, I situate my body in a position of stillness. I take a few deep breaths. I turn my palms downward resting on my thighs. As I do this, I imagine placing my palms in God's hands. I thank Him for whatever comes to my mind and spirit. Then I turn my palms upward in a position of receptivity, asking God to give me whatever my heart needs today.

Prayer

My loving God, I thank You that You provide both a hunger for You and deep satisfaction in You. Help me to be fully present and open to the splendor of a vital life with You. Amen.

Story of the Day

Then came the day of Unleavened Bread on which the Passover lamb had to be sacrificed. Jesus sent Peter and John, saying, "Go and make preparations for us to eat the Passover."

"Where do you want us to prepare for it?" they asked.

He replied, "As you enter the city, a man carrying a jar of water will meet you. Follow him to the house that he enters, and say to the owner of the house, 'The Teacher asks: Where is the guest room, where I may eat the Passover with my disciples?' He will show you a large room upstairs, all furnished. Make preparations there."

They left and found things just as Jesus had told them. So they prepared the Passover.

When the hour came, Jesus and his apostles reclined at the table. And he said to them, "I have eagerly desired to eat this Passover with you before I suffer. For I tell you, I will not eat it again until it finds fulfillment in the kingdom of God."

After taking the cup, he gave thanks and said, "Take this and divide it among you. For I tell you I will not drink again from the fruit of the vine until the kingdom of God comes."

And he took bread, gave thanks and broke it, and gave it to them, saying, "This is my body given for you; do this in remembrance of me."

In the same way, after the supper he took the cup, saying, "This cup is the new covenant in my blood, which is poured out for you. But the hand of him who is going to betray me is with mine on the table. The Son of Man will go as it has been decreed. But woe to that man who betrays him!" They began to question among themselves which of them it might be who would do this.

A dispute also arose among them as to which of them was considered to be greatest (Luke 22:7-24).

Entering the Scene

It is Passover, the Jewish feast commemorating God's deliverance from Egypt. On this night Jesus will reveal that He is the divine liberator anticipated in the Passover feast—the long-awaited Lamb of God come to deliver us from the slavery of sin. At long last, the Passover has found its fulfillment.

Have you ever wanted to give a gift to someone dear so much that it was hard to wait? That is Jesus tonight. He is overflowing with excitement and longing, "I have eagerly desired to eat this Passover with you before I suffer" (Luke 22:15). His heart aches for union with His disciples as never before.

Yes, tonight is the last supper with His disciples and the first New Covenant meal rooted in the unconditional love of God. It is the last meal Jesus will share with His beloved disciples until He raises the cup again to celebrate with His Bride, the Church, on the day of their wedding feast. Can you feel the weight and depth of Jesus' gift?

Yet, how is His gift received? "Of all the meals the Lord must have shared with them, this was the one that should have gone beautifully and perfectly; it did not. From one moment to the next the blows just got worse. There were inept responses, distractions, bullheaded debates, and rebukes directed against Jesus...and then of course betrayal. It was nothing short of a disaster. . . . There was squabbling, misunderstanding, argumentativeness, and betrayal, all packed in one evening. . . . Watch how things begin with the loving and careful attentiveness of the Lord and end with a selfish, inept, and unloving response from the Apostles (us)."[5]

Place yourself in this scene. How do you feel? Do you wish to say anything to the disciples?

It's chaos, but Jesus proceeds. Pressing through distractions and hardened hearts, Jesus "looks into the cup at His own blood, soon to be shed, and He distributes His own body, soon to be handed over."[6] Catch the expression on Jesus's face. What do you read there? Jesus hands Himself over to His friends saying, "take, eat and drink." He is not inviting them to ponder, study, or try these gifts. Instead His message is bold and explicit, "Embrace My body with the strength of both of your hands. Relish and feed on Me. Take hold of this cup of salvation. Discover the power of My blood with your utmost determination and passion."

When your turn comes, how do you receive these precious gifts?

Meanwhile, the disciples are oblivious to the miracle that has just taken place. They resume fighting and arguing. When Judas walks out, nobody notices, cares, or holds him back.

Going Deeper

Is this why Jesus emphasizes our *remembering* and *repeating* the events of that night? He knows that we have a tendency to forget His great love, especially when we are consumed by our own misgivings. It's like He is saying, "After I leave . . . just keep repeating this until I come again, and the deep message will slowly sink in until 'the bride' is fully ready to meet 'the bridegroom' and drink at the eternal wedding feast."[7] The Last Supper has been an utter disaster but Jesus trusts us. He trusts that one day His followers will discover what it all means. He invites all His disciples to practice the unceasing memory of His love.

Does Jesus' patience give us hope when we are not being heard, when children ignore what's being said, when co-workers snicker, when the preacher's message is not received?

Perhaps one day, when the time is ripe, they will remember!

Just recently I met a woman who has remembered well the sacrifice of Jesus and discovered the preciousness of His blood and body. Throughout her journey with cancer, the celebration of Holy Communion has been her daily sustenance. "I know that Jesus Christ is truly alive and present in the Holy Eucharist. I often ask, 'Oh Jesus, as Your Blood mingles with mine and flows through my body, heal any cancer cells that You might find; please heal my thyroid and my gut as You pass by. Thank You, Sweet Jesus. How I love, adore, and praise You!"

With what kind of hope do you receive the body and blood of our Lord?

The words of Jesus remind me of the miracle of blood transfusion. Our contemporary understanding of what occurs as blood is transfused unfolds the intended meaning of Jesus. In his book, *In His Image*[8] Dr. Paul Brand describes the night that he, as a young medical student, witnessed the resurrection of a young women. She had come into the emergency room pale, drained of life, her pulse weak, and her breathing shallow. Dr. Brand connected her to a supply of blood and watched as her face slowly regained color. Her eyes fluttered open to gaze up into his. Within just minutes, the infusion of blood had restored her so that she was able to sit up in bed. How does this story speak to you about the meaning of the Lord's Supper where Jesus transfuses us with *His* blood, infusing us with His life, power, and strength?

Impressions of Jesus's Heart for Your Journey

My friend, it is impossible to imitate Me outside the bond of unity. Allow Me to abide in you and fully share life with you. "Very truly I tell you, unless you eat the flesh of the Son of Man and drink his blood, you have no life in you. Whoever eats my flesh and drinks my blood has eternal life, and I will raise them up at the last day. For my flesh is real food and my blood is real drink. Whoever eats my flesh and drinks my blood remains in me, and I in them" (John 6:53-56).

Your Response

Notice what you are feeling right now. Let these feelings, whatever they might be, draw you into a vocal or written conversation with the Lord.

In prayer for you,
Liena

Victory Over Fear

Dear Friend,

Has there been time when you stood at the crossroad of decision, knowing what you should do yet feeling completely paralyzed with fear and dread? Come and walk with Jesus today. Allow His agony and victory to teach you the way through fear into the freedom of surrender.

Preparing to Reflect

I make myself comfortable in my prayer chair. I relax my shoulders and allow the tension to drain from my body. I release any sense of uneasiness and gently tell myself, "I am here to be understood." I remember that "Now that we know what we have—Jesus, this great High Priest with ready access to God—let's not let it slip through our fingers. We don't have a priest who is out of touch with our reality. He's been through weakness and testing, experienced it all—all but the sin. So let's walk right up to him and get what he is ready to give. Take the mercy, accept the help" (Hebrew 4:14-16 MSG). I lean into Jesus and tell Him what I need; I surrender to Him.

Prayer

Today, O Lord, I yield myself to You.
May Your will be my delight today.
May You have perfect sway in me.
May Your love be the pattern of my living.
I surrender to You my hopes, my dreams, my ambitions.
Do with them what You will, when You will, and as You will.
I place into Your loving care my family, my friends, my future.

Care for them with a care I can never give.

I release into Your hands my need to control, my craving for status, my fear of obscurity.

Eradicate the evil, purify the good, and establish Your Kingdom on earth.

For Jesus' sake, Amen.

Richard Foster[9]

Story of the Day

And they come to a piece of land called Gethsemane and [Jesus] says to his disciples, "Sit here while I pray." And He takes Peter, James, and John with Him and He begins to go into shock and be overcome. And He says to them, "I feel so utterly sad that I could die. Stay here and keep watch. "And going on a little further He collapsed onto the ground and He prayed that if it were possible, the Hour might pass Him by. He was saying, "ABBA, Father, all things are possible for you; take way this cup from Me; yet not as I will, but as You will." And He comes and finds [the disciples] sleeping. And He says to Peter, "Simon, are you sleeping? Do you not have the strength to keep watch for a single hour? Keep watch and pray so that you may not enter into temptation. The spirit is eager, but the flesh is weak." And going away He prayed, using the same expression. And coming a second time He found them sleeping, for their eyes were very heavy. They did not know how to answer Him. And He comes a third time and says to them, "You can sleep from now on and take your rest; it is all over. The Hour has come, and behold, the Son of Man is betrayed into the hands of the sinners. Rise. Let us go forth. Behold the one which is betraying Me approaches" (Mark 14:32-42, Translation by Michael Casey).[10]

Entering the Scene

It is a blessing not to know everything about tomorrow. Were we to know what is coming, we might not have the courage to face it.

But Jesus *knows*. He knows exactly what is going to happen to Him. *That* is the difference. Jesus sees His betrayer approaching. He feels the whip of the Roman soldiers slashing His skin. He feels the weight of His broken body hanging on the tree. Worst of all, He anticipates the agony of being separated from the Father and Spirit. He feels it all.

Jesus' despair rises with the force of a tsunami. He knows that there is only one solution to His great need: *prayer*. He has to be transformed and strengthened to face this horror. So, Jesus forms two prayer rings around Himself. First, He brings very close His friends, Peter, James, and John. He asks them to keep a prayer vigil, surrounding Him in a circle of protection. These three men were present when Jesus was transfigured on the mountain. They know Him. The King of the Universe pleads for their compassion and support, "Keep watch with Me; I am going into shock right now and could die."

Upon witnessing our Lord's breakdown, His stunned companions withdraw. They separate themselves from His pain. The disciples plunge into the sea of forgetfulness and denial. They check out and fall asleep, "exhausted from sorrow" (Luke 22:45). Have you ever been exhausted from sorrow? While the disciples are sleeping, can you keep watch with Jesus?

The Son of God stumbles away into the distance. As His knees hit the ground Jesus once created, blood rolls like streams of sweat down His body, soaking the dirt bright scarlet. Gethsemane means *the oil press*. Behold, the Son of God is crushed to become the healing oil for all humanity. Kneel beside Him, touch His shuddering body, hear His cry of relinquishment, "Abba, Father, all things are possible for You. Take away this cup away from Me; nevertheless, not what I will, but what You will" (Mark 14:36 NKJV).

Silence. Jesus feels weak and desperate. He struggles to His feet in search of the companionship of His friends. "Are they still with me? Are they interceding?" He wonders. Only a few steps away Jesus stumbles upon His slumbering disciples. The terror of death sweeps our Lord up again in the tempest of panic. He begs them to intercede on His behalf then rushes back to prayer two more times. When it seems that no one, absolutely no one, stands beside Him, an angel of His heavenly Father comes to enfold Him in heaven's embrace. "An angel from heaven appeared to him and strengthened him" (Luke 22:43).

Going Deeper

What is it like for you to witness the wrestling of Jesus? What is the source of His grave distress?

As is true of all of us, Jesus experiences the weakness of the flesh: *fear*. In the garden, He is confronted by the human temptation to flee in the presence of overwhelming opposition. The devil has returned to tempt Jesus and draw Him away from the Father's will. Luke writes at the end of Jesus' temptation in the desert, "When the devil had finished all this tempting, he left him until an opportune time" (Luke 4:13). The hour of crisis and more opportune time has come.

Notice what Jesus does in His weakness. He falls into prayer, the *only* source of strength and transformation. Knowing that this is His battle, Jesus removes Himself from His friends, but at the same time, He longs for their support. Let's listen to how He prays, let us learn, from Him, how we may follow His example in times of crisis.

First, Jesus reaffirms His relationship with His Father. In the teeth of the storm, Jesus anchors Himself in the bond of affection. Listen and repeat aloud with Him several times, "Abba Father" ("Daddy" or "my loving Father"). How does repeating this affirmation affect you?

Second, Jesus confesses His faith in God, "all things are possible to You." Crisis tends to put blinders on our vision; it corners us and seeks to persuade us that all hope is lost. Jesus chooses to open and extend His frightened heart to embrace His confidence in God's endless possibilities. Confessing God's limitless power unbolts the shutters of our soul to let in the fresh air of God's loving creativity.

We notice that a confession of faith is Jesus' common way of praying. Before Lazurus' tomb we hear Jesus pray, "Father, I thank you that you heard me. I knew that you always hear me" (John 11:41-42). Imagine how our faith would change if we would always come to Abba saying, "Thank You that You always hear me. Thank You that all things are possible for You."

Third, Jesus expresses the raw truth before His Father. "The boldness of faith does not allow us to dissimulate our real needs or to hide our desires under a cloak of respectability. With God who knows the heart, our only approach must be direct and unabashed. We are to pray for what we desire, without first working things out in our head. Jesus prays from the trepidation in which he is plunged, asking in all simplicity to be delivered from the fate that looms ahead of him. If all things are possible to God, no prayer is inappropriate."[11]

Do you tend to work things out in your head before praying? Or do you just tell the truth of your heart to your Father?

Fourth, Jesus' prayer flows into the most powerful word: "yet". It is not the "yet" of a weakened faith (I never get what I pray anyhow); it is not resignation, nor is it the "yet" of hopelessness. Jesus' "yet" is an affirmation of a possibility that is higher, wider, and deeper than His own ideas, vision, or pressing need. The "yet" of Jesus confesses His faith in the Father's superb wisdom, comprehensive plan, and love for all humanity. Jesus' "yet" *rests* in the ultimate goodness of Abba Father.

Jesus returns to the same prayer three times in the garden, indicating that He is in the process of transformation, He is working through His crisis. Notice that the circumstance of His situation does not change. The betrayer is still on his way; the cross yet looms before Him. However, Jesus emerges from His prayer transformed, like a warrior prepared for battle. He is resolved. His stamina has returned. "The crisis has passed, even though the torment has yet to begin."[12] Jesus takes charge of the situation.

While embracing a challenging resolution in your life, have you ever experienced a similar transformation? Jesus shows us that prayer is first and foremost a place of *conversion and change.* Might Jesus, through His journey, be challenging us to approach every prayer time with this same mindset? "I am coming to You, Abba, for a change of heart according to the need of my situation."

Impressions of Jesus's Heart for Your Journey

My sister and My brother, I understand you. I kneel beside you in *your* Gethsemane. I desire to strengthen you in your hour of temptation and resolve to follow our Father's will. Let Me come alongside you. Remember, "My grace is sufficient for you, for My strength is made perfect in weakness" (2 Corinthians 12:9 NKJV).

Your Response

How is your spirit stirred after today's meditation and prayer? What do you want to say to Jesus who has walked in your shoes?

May the Lord bless you and keep you,
Your companion,
Liena

The Power of Silence

Dear Pilgrim,

Have you ever been the victim of a bully? Has someone maligned your reputation or accused you of something for which you are innocent? Then you know something of what Jesus endured on Thursday evening and Friday morning as the long hours of His passion commenced. In His response to accusations, Jesus shows us how to respond when we are the victim of persecution.

Preparing to Reflect

> *The Sovereign LORD has spoken to me,*
> *   and I have listened.*
> *   I have not rebelled or turned away.*
> *I offered my back to those who beat me*
> *   and my cheeks to those who pulled out my beard.*
> *I did not hide my face*
> *   from mockery and spitting.*
> *Because the Sovereign Lord helps me,*
> *   I will not be disgraced.*
> *Therefore, I have set my face like a stone,*
> *   determined to do His will.*
> *   And I know that I will not be put to shame.*
>
> Isaiah 50: 5-7 NLT

I take a moment to meditate on these words from Scripture. I listen to my heart. Is there a wounded place crying out for the help and vindication of God? I bring it before the Lord in prayer.

Prayer

Lord Jesus Christ, I come to You today as One who knows what it is to be unfairly maligned. I desire to respond to this injury as You would in my place, so please give me the grace of humility and show me how to respond. This I ask in Your name. Amen.

Story of the Day

Early in the morning, all the chief priests and the elders of the people made their plans how to have Jesus executed. So they bound him, led him away and handed him over to Pilate, the governor.

Meanwhile Jesus stood before the governor, and the governor asked him, "Are you the king of the Jews?"

"You have said so," Jesus replied.

When he was accused by the chief priest and the elders, he gave no answer. Then Pilate asked him, "Don't you hear the testimony they are bringing against you?" But Jesus made no reply, not even a single charge—to the great amazement of the governor (Matthew 27:1-2, 11-14).

Entering the Scene

There have been many sleepless nights in human history, but none like this. Jesus stands the whole night in unbroken silence before the Jewish leaders. They accuse Him, question Him, shout at Him, and fabricate lies about Him. The hurricane of falsehood rages against the impenetrable stillness of the Lord. The only answer they get is Jesus' eyes piercing them with truth.

Is Jesus alone? No. Jesus stands with all innocent children whose deaths scandalize us and with all the martyrs of all times who die in powerful silence. He is companioned by all who can't or choose not to defend themselves against evil. The silence of the innocent on the earth is a cry answered in heaven.

Place yourself in this room. How would you describe this incredible tension of many hours? For a moment imagine being Jesus. What's is it like? And then imagine being a Jewish leader. What are you experiencing?

The chief priest and the elders, in justifying themselves, bind the unresisting Lord as though He were a dangerous criminal. Stay with this emerging paradox for a while. "His bound hands hold back the legions of angels."[13]

The Jewish leaders lead the silent and exhausted Lamb of God to the judgment seat of Pilate. This is so profoundly significant. At the same exact time the chief priests are busy reciting the morning liturgy of the Tamid sacrifice and the compulsory sacred assembly of the first day of the Feast of Unleavened Bread in the Jerusalem temple, the unblemished Lamb of God is tied near the altar for everyone to judge *His* perfection before the High Priest, Joseph Caiaphas. Caiaphas pronounces the sacrificial lamb "without fault" and suitable for sacrifice. What meaning do you sense in these parallel events? What does God want you to understand?

Unease grips Pilate when his eyes meet those of the prisoner, Jesus. Pilate has never seen anyone respond like Him. Pilate is used to hysteria, pleading, anger, and the despair of criminals. He can deal with all of that, but the silence of Jesus and His brief acknowledgment that He is the King of the Jews puts Pilate momentarily off-balance. Place yourself in Pilate's shoes for a minute. What would be your response to Jesus' silence and His startling claim?

> He was oppressed and He was afflicted,
> Yet He opened not His mouth;
> He was led as a lamb to the slaughter,
> And as a sheep before its shearers is silent,
> So He opened not His mouth.
>
> Isaiah 53:7 NKJV

Going Deeper

Sometimes remaining silent reveals God's power more than speaking out. Whatever can elicit a response from us has power over us. That is why bullies try to rile their victims. If they can get the other person to become angry, sad, or even retaliate in kind, the bully feels powerful; he has forced the other person to do what he wants. You know who has power over you by who is "making" you do what they want you to do.

Jesus demonstrates in His behavior before the Jewish leaders and Governor Pilate that sometimes silence is the greatest display of power. Jesus shows the world the power of God through His words and deeds, but also through His silence. He does not defend Himself. He doesn't have to. He doesn't proclaim His innocence. He doesn't have to. He just stands His ground in silence.

Richard Foster challenged a gathering of pastors, missionaries, and Christian authors to "clothe yourselves with humility." He explained that we can only "go to the wall" for one person's reputation. "You can either make it all about Jesus," Richard said, "or you can make it about yourself, but you cannot have it both ways. The minute you shift the focus from Jesus to establish or defend your own reputation, you take center-stage." Richard told the group that as Christian leaders they never have the right to defend or seek to vindicate themselves. "When you make the decision to follow Jesus," he said, "you set aside your own reputation to defend His." Richard concluded by saying that the best action to take when maligned is to leave the matter in God's hands and remain silent.

Isn't this what we see Jesus doing in the trial for His life? He leaves His reputation and well-being in the hands of the Father; He refuses to mount a defense on His own behalf.

Jesus, the Lamb of God, submits willingly to death because He knows it is the only way to secure our freedom; it is the only way He can guarantee being together with us for all eternity. "Father, I want those you have given me to be with me where I am, and to see my glory, the glory you have given me (John 17:24).

In the nineteenth century, Joseph Scriven wrote a popular hymn entitled, "What a Friend We Have in Jesus." A verse declares,

O what peace we often forfeit,
O what needless pain we bear,

All because we do not carry
Everything to God in prayer.[14]

How is Jesus calling you to stand with Him in silence, trusting Him for your ultimate vindication? Talk with Jesus about this.

Impressions of Jesus' Heart for Your Journey

Dear One, I know what it feels like when your reputation is being sullied. I came to My own people, and they received Me not (see John 1:11). They spit on Me, punched Me in the face, abused Me, and even accused Me of slandering My heavenly Father. But I knew that the Father was with Me, so I answered nothing. Trust Me with your reputation. Trust Me to bring you through the flood and fire. Trust Me that in the end, all shall be well.

Your Response

Ponder how God might be inviting you to handle hurtful accusations and attacks in the manner of Jesus. What is the prayer arising from your new awareness? Journal your thoughts to Jesus.

May the peace of God guard your heart,
Your loving Lent friend,
Liena

Clash of Expectations

My Lent Companion,

Unmet expectations can really hurt and disorient us. They can confuse us to the point of disillusionment, bitterness, fear, silent despair, and even rage. Today we witness this occurring in the crowd screaming, "Crucify him! Crucify him!"

Have you been in that place where your expectations and dreams seem to clash with God's intentions? How do you go about it? Today's story speaks loudly of this human dilemma. What are the lessons to be learned?

Preparing to Reflect

Prayer is a homecoming from all my distractions, wonderings, concerns, worries, and scatteredness to the center of my being where God waits for me to meet all my needs.

I let myself dwell for a moment on God's life-giving presence within me and ask for the help of the Holy Spirit to bring me "home."

Prayer

Everlasting Father, You are my true home, my true center, and my true shelter. I hide and rest in Thee. Amen.

Story of the Day

During the feast the governor was accustomed to release one prisoner to the crowd, whomever they wanted. At that time they had in custody a notorious prisoner named Jesus Barabbas. So after they had assembled, Pilate said to them, "Whom do you want me to release for you, Jesus

Barabbas or Jesus who is called the Christ?" (For he knew that they had handed him over because of envy.) As he was sitting on the judgment seat, his wife sent a message to him: "Have nothing to do with that innocent man; I have suffered greatly as a result of a dream about him today." But the chief priests and the elders persuaded the crowds to ask for Barabbas and to have Jesus killed. The governor asked them, "Which of the two do you want me to release for you?" And they said, "Barabbas!" Pilate said to them, "Then what should I do with Jesus who is called the Christ?" They all said, "Crucify him!" He asked, "Why? What wrong has he done?" But they shouted more insistently, "Crucify him!"

When Pilate saw that he could do nothing, but that instead a riot was starting, he took some water, washed his hands before the crowd and said, "I am innocent of this man's blood. You take care of it yourselves!" In reply all the people said, "Let his blood be on us and on our children!" Then he released Barabbas for them. But after he had Jesus flogged, he handed him over to be crucified (Matthew 27:15-26 NET).

Entering the Scene

The chief priests and the elders rile the crowd, convincing people, "Demand to crucify him! Put him to death! Crucify him! Crucify him!" Even those who recognize Jesus' innocence succumb to their leaders' influence. To out-scream their conscience, people shout even louder, "Crucify him!"

Place yourself in this scene. How are you affected by the raging crowd? What are you impelled to do?

Now empathize with Jesus, standing alone before the multitude. "All around Him, filling His ears, filling His mind, half defeating Him, the cries of the crowd break over Him like the waves of a sea in a storm, a sea in which it would seem impossible to be drowned. They are cries of derision, of hatred, of disappointment, of despair, despair with a note of accusation against Him; cries of contempt; cries which could, and would, drown the soul of anyone who loved less than He loves, who knew less of human nature than He knows."[15] Pilate is caught between preserving peace in his city and his strong sense of Jesus' innocence. Feel for a moment his tension. Even his wife is persuaded of Jesus's blamelessness in her torturous dreams. What an irony: that only a Gentile Roman and his wife recognize Jesus' innocence. Seemingly out of options, Pilate lets the crowd choose between releasing the criminal, Jesus Barabbas, or Jesus the Christ. Pilate washes his hands of responsibility while the crowd blindly welcomes the curse, "Let his blood be on us and on our children!" (Matthew 27:25 NET).

Going Deeper

How comfortable are you with a vulnerable and woundable God? The people of Jerusalem are not. They reject the concept of a peaceful king. For them Jesus has become useless, unable to carry out their expectations of political freedom. They are disgusted with Him. How does He dare to give up the fight, not use His supernatural power, and stand there silent before Pilate? What a failure. What a reject. "Crucify him! Crucify Him! Give us Jesus Barabbas who can make life right again!"

How about our personal moments of deep disappointment? You probably can recall a time in your life when you realized that something was not going to happen. That sinking feeling that "he or she will not live," the fear that "my cancer will not be cured," that "I will never be a father or a mother," that "she or he will never change," that "I will be unable to fulfill this mission," that "this marriage will not survive." How do you keep your bleeding heart open and engaged in these dire circumstances?

Only love for God is not deceived by *the way things look* but *keeps* following Jesus to the grave where we experience the miracle of resurrection. We witness this assurance in Mary Magdalene and in the other women who followed Jesus. *Only* love intuits God's veiled but loving intentions and pulls us forward to discover life after the death of a cherished dream.

I like to meditate on the concept of God's left-handed and right-handed power. The concept of left-handed power was introduced by Martin Luther. The right hand represents straight-line power—the mighty and direct acts of God. One could say that all Jesus' healings and miracles were performed by the right hand of God. Left-handed power signifies the power that moves through mystery, paradox, and suffering. "Left-handed power, in other words, is precisely paradoxical power: power that looks for all the world like weakness, intervention that seems indistinguishable from non-intervention. Which may not, at first glance, seem like much of a thing to insure, let alone like an exercise worthy of the name power. But when you come to think of it, it is power—so much power, in fact, that it is the only thing in the world that evil can't touch."[16]

Have you ever been very disappointed in God's right hand not moving, only to discover that His *left hand* has been all along guiding you through the valley of shadow and death?

If you ask people to name the time in their life when they felt the closest to God, most refer to a time when they endured pain or significant loss. At the time their suffering was at its greatest, an experience they hope never to repeat. But looking back through the lens of what God accomplished *through* their suffering, they admit that they wouldn't trade the experience for anything.

Impressions of Jesus' Heart for Your Journey

You are My beloved and I desire to carry you on My back through any valley of death and loss. "Let the beloved of the LORD rest secure in him, for he shields him all day long, and the one the LORD loves rests between his shoulders" (Deuteronomy 33:12).

Your Response

What is your response to Jesus' invitation to rest between His shoulders?

Praying for your highest good,
Liena

_____

_____

_____

_____

_____

_____

_____

_____

_____

_____

_____

_____

_____

_____

_____

_____

_____

_____

_____

_____

_____

_____

_____

_____

_____

What is God's Vision for You?

Dear Lent Pilgrim,

Recall a time in your life when you recognized the deception of your heart and were utterly disappointed in yourself. That's Peter in today's story. How does Jesus bring him out of this disparaging place? Come and discover Jesus' presence and intentions in the midst of your own failures and fall.

Preparing to Reflect

In the silence of this moment, I become mindful of God's presence with me. I take a few deep breaths and allow God's loving gaze to rest upon me as I center down to pray.

I recall the story of a blind beggar sitting on the roadside. When he realizes that Jesus is passing by, he starts yelling, "Jesus, Son of David, have mercy on me!" (Luke 18:38). Jesus stops, becomes still, and tries to locate him. I imagine now Jesus becoming still for me, turning His face toward me, and asking, "What can I do for you?" What is your answer?

Prayer

Jesus, Son of the Living God, have mercy on me a sinner. Amen.

Story of the Day

Then seizing him, they led him away and took him into the house of the high priest. Peter followed at a distance. And when some there had kindled a fire in the middle of the courtyard and had sat down together, Peter sat down with them. A servant girl saw him seated there in the firelight. She looked closely at him and said, "This man was with him."

But he denied it. "Woman, I don't know him," he said.

A little later someone else saw him and said, "You also are one of them."

"Man, I am not!" Peter replied.

About an hour later another asserted, "Certainly this fellow was with him, for he is a Galilean."

Peter replied, "Man, I don't know what you're talking about!" Just as he was speaking, the rooster crowed. The Lord turned and looked straight at Peter. Then Peter remembered the word the Lord had spoken to him: "Before the rooster crows today, you will disown me three times." And he went outside and wept bitterly (Luke 22:54-62).

Entering the Scene

When Jesus was with Peter, nothing seemed impossible. In all sincerity Peter swore, "Lord, I am ready to go with you to prison and to death" (Luke 22:33). But as soon as the Lord is arrested, Peter's courage vanishes in Jesus' absence. Does Peter even recognize himself in his denial?

Do you remember a time you were confronted with the duplicity of your own heart?

All Peter can do is to follow Jesus from a distance. As the night deepens, Peter is chilled to the bone. He squeezes himself in by the fire. If you could be there with him, what would you see? What is Peter's face telling you? I see him nervously rubbing his hands, bouncing from one foot to the other, nervous, and shaken by fear. His thoughts are in utter disarray. An accusing voice startles Peter to awareness, "You also were with Jesus of Galilee" (Mathew 26:69). Peter plays stupid and blurts back, "I don't know what you are talking about" (Matthew 26:70).

Denial of Jesus thrusts Peter into a free fall, unstoppable by his own will. His soul drops into hellish darkness with each successive *no*—"I don't know that man," "I don't know that man!"—until the rooster crows and Jesus catches Peter in his free fall with one piercing look.

In a single stroke, Jesus *convicts* and *loves* Peter. "This combination, of being utterly known, yet unconditionally loved, is the only true liber ation. The truth really does set us free."[17]

Realizing what he has done, Peter flees the courtyard in sobs of contrition. Follow Peter. What do you witness?

Going Deeper

Peter runs from the others and from himself, overcome with remorse, shame, and self-loathing—just as Judas did earlier that same night. But what is the difference between them? Peter cries holy tears of penitence and is washed with God's grace. Judas cries unholy tears of dejection and drowns in hopeless despair.

When Peter is about to give up, he remembers the words of Jesus, "Simon, Simon, Satan has asked to sift all of you as wheat. But I have prayed for you, Simon, that your faith may not fail. And when you have turned back, strengthen your brothers" (Luke 22:31-32). What might have happened had Peter not had these words to fall back on? Might he have been tempted to end his life as did Judas?

The importance of speaking prophetically into each other's lives is priceless. Have you ever been utterly discouraged, but then remembered someone's love for you and their affirmative words?

Graham Cooke notes that just before He is arrested, Jesus speaks from the future into Peter's present circumstance so that Peter, after his repentance, can inherit a clear pathway to follow. "God speaks to us prophetically about our future and then relates to us in the present through our destiny. God begins to develop us from the place of our future toward where we are in the present."[18] Jesus does not live in denial about Peter or us. Jesus knows exactly the propensity of Peter's heart, but He does not permit Peter to get stuck in his present situation. He prays for Peter and points to his true identity and future.

How dedicated are we to affirm people's gifting and identity in Christ so that when they fall into despair they will remember our words of affirmation and reject Satan's harsh condemnation? I will always remember getting my first job after coming to America. My employer assured me, "If you make a mistake, you will be forgiven." His kindness inspired me.

Whereas Judas received a dismissive, cold look from the Jewish elders and chief priests after his confession (Matthew 27:4), Peter was saved by the power of a simple gaze from Jesus. Jesus looked at Peter with love *through* and *beyond* Peter's sin and despair. That single look simultaneously *broke* and *healed* Peter's heart. Jesus' ministry of gaze is so impactful that Peter applies it later on in his own ministry. In Acts 3:1-10 we read about Peter healing a crippled beggar. Peter looks straight at him, as does John, and says, "Look at us!" (Acts 3:4). So, the man gives them his attention and receives healing in Jesus' name.

"Peter and John have no silver or gold to give him. Healing comes for the crippled beggar as Peter and John read his face, as they gaze upon him with an invitation to look upon them in return—a face-to-face look of love. In this encounter, the suffering one allows his nothingness and nakedness to seen by others in the epiphany of his face. And in that light—that is love—a possibility for new life emerges that can only be seen, and received, as a gift."[19]

The Holy Spirit indwells us; we are the living icons of God. Never underestimate God's desire to disperse His light and healing into this world through *your* eyes. The way we look at people is crucial. Do you believe in the power and ministry of *your* gaze?

In my work as a chaplain I rely on God seeing people through me. When encountering people in hysteria and sheer madness, I urge them, "Look at me!" I trust the Lord to seize them with His peace. If someone's suffering is too great for my words to console them, I simply let my loving gaze rest upon them. I trust the Lord to comfort them.

Do you believe that Jesus' look through you can be enough to heal someone in your path? If you doubt, why?

"By looking long and lovingly into the face of suffering, we might learn to really see by a love that knows how to really look." We are called to behold each other in the same way God beholds us.

Impressions of Jesus' Heart for Your Journey

My dear child, I pray for you as I prayed for Peter with your future and transformation in My mind. Don't allow any failure to hold you back from the future I envision for you. "For I know the plans I have for you, . . . plans for your welfare and not for calamity to give you a future and a hope" (Jeremiah 29:11 NASB).

Your Response

Feel the strength of Jesus' love for you. How do you want to respond to His affection today? Voice or journal your intentions.

Lent blessings,
Your sister in Christ,
Liena

The Fourth Week of Lent

Judas Come Home— All is Forgiven!

Shalom,

"I have been betrayed." Have you muttered these words at one time or another? Betrayal shakes us at the core of our being and robs us of a sense of security. It leaves us vulnerable.

Or maybe you have betrayed someone and are still dealing with a deep sense of remorse. Either way, the relationship of Judas and Jesus gives us deep insight into the complexities of disloyalty. Come and explore with me the path of healing.

Preparing to Reflect

My attention is the most awaited gift God desires to receive from me. I prepare my body to be relaxed and at ease. I take a few minutes to still myself in God's presence and to appreciate His faithfulness to me as I meditate on the following experience. "In crushing circumstances, I learned about the constancy of the Lord. I began to grasp the idea that whatever He is, He is relentless. He is massively, enormously, incredibly unchanging. His love is ceaseless, endless and everlasting. His great heart is fixed, steadfast and immovable. He became my North Star."[1]

I never have to wonder where God stands with me. His heart toward me is unchangingly loving. "If we are faithless, he remains faithful, for he cannot disown himself" (2 Timothy2:13). What do these words mean to you personally?

Prayer

Loving Father, Lord Jesus Christ, and indwelling Holy Spirit, I praise

You for Your permanent faithfulness and love for me. I thank You for the everlasting rest, peace, and safety Your faithfulness provides. Amen.

Story of the Day

Then one of the Twelve—the one called Judas Iscariot—went to the chief priests and asked, "What are you willing to give me if I deliver him over to you?" So they counted out for him thirty pieces of silver. From then on Judas watched for an opportunity to hand him over (Matthew 26:14-16).

Jesus was troubled in spirit and testified, "Very truly I tell you, one of you is going to betray me."

His disciples stared at one another, at a loss to know which of them he meant. One of them, the disciple whom Jesus loved, was reclining next to him. Simon Peter motioned to this disciple and said, "Ask him which one he means."

Leaning back against Jesus, he asked him, "Lord, who is it?"

Jesus answered, "It is the one to whom I will give this piece of bread when I have dipped it in the dish." Then, dipping the piece of bread, he gave it to Judas, the son of Simon Iscariot. As soon as Judas took the bread, Satan entered into him.

So Jesus told him, "What you are about to do, do quickly." But no one at the meal understood why Jesus said this to him. Since Judas had charge of the money, some thought Jesus was telling him to buy what was needed for the festival, or to give something to the poor. As soon as Judas had taken the bread, he went out. And it was night (John 13:21-30).

While he was still speaking, Judas, one of the Twelve, arrived. With him was a large crowd armed with swords and clubs, sent from the chief priests and the elders of the people. Now the betrayer had arranged a signal with them: "The one I kiss is the man; arrest him." Going at once to Jesus, Judas said, "Greetings, Rabbi!" and kissed him (Matthew 26:47-49).

Entering the Scene

Throughout the years Judas has cultivated the sin of stealing, and now the devil takes full advantage of this well-established vise to use Judas for his will. The powerful compulsion to have more money takes hold of Judas. The strong impulse pulls him into the raging current of no return. Obsessed, driven, and stealthy, Judas makes his way to the house of the chief priests. His mind is fixed upon one consuming thought, "I wonder how much they will give me for Jesus?"

Judas stumbles further and further away from God in a world of delusion and excuses. Can you see the evil muttering in the heart of Judas? "This rabbi Jesus is an absolute failure and letdown. He has not started a rebellion against Rome, and he never will. He is not the messiah we were expecting. Better get something out of this disappointment." Judas rehearses these lies until in his mind Jesus is diminished to nothing. He sells our Lord for thirty pieces of silver, the price of a slave. Satan succeeds in tempting Judas to *self-redeem* a disappointing situation through greed and grasping.

Afterward Judas makes his way back to the other disciples and Jesus who are gathered around the Last Supper. Imagine yourself sitting among them. What do you see in the eyes of Judas when he enters the room and takes the place of honor?

Jesus dips bread in the bitter herbs and hands it to Judas. Judas' outstretched hand confirms his intent. Judas accepts Satan's charge to betray Jesus. With a single gesture a bread of union becomes a bread of deceit. Fully possessed by evil, Judas recedes in utter darkness.

The ill-treating of agape meal leads to betraying Jesus with a kiss in the garden of Gethsemane. Shortly thereafter Judas' eyes are uncovered, as were those of Eve and Adam, to recognize that he is in the wrong. Where will he hide? In this dire moment, the devil convinces Judas that he can never be forgiven this great sin. Satan always *uses* and *disposes* of people. Judas, utterly alone, chooses to "self-redeem" the situation by hanging himself on the tree.

Going Deeper

From the day Jesus calls Judas to follow Him until the day Judas betrays Him, Jesus never changes His attitude toward this disciple. Jesus treats him the same as the other followers. Judas eats and sleeps with Jesus and walks beside Him. Along with the other disciples, Judas receives the authority to cast out demons and heal the sick. Judas witnesses Jesus' miracles and he shares the Last Supper with the Lord. Jesus washes his feet. Even when Judas' lips burn Jesus' face with the kiss of betrayal, Christ turns to Judas and calls him a friend. Jesus is not sarcastic, He *remains true* to His relationship with Judas. When Jesus says, "Love your enemy," He truly does. Jesus is the same yesterday, today, and tomorrow.

What does being constant in all of your relationships mean to you? Albert Day describes God's changelessness in the most beautiful way.

When we say that God is holy, we are not naming an attribute among many others such as love and mercy and wisdom and power. We are attempting to designate something that applies to all His attributes, something that gives them an awesome dimension. We are saying that He is the changeless One. His love never fluctuates; His mercy is inexhaustible; His wisdom cherishes all that is truly good; His power can always be trusted to act redemptively. The supreme wonder and unrivalled glory is that He is all that He is, unchangeably. "In Him is no variableness" is the New Testament assurance. So we need not speculate what will be His response whenever we turn to Him, whether it be from an hour of victory or from a night of defeat. . . . Sometimes the best of us have days when our dearest friends must say, "you are not yourself today." That fact gives them a hard time and sends them away deprived of what they should have from us. BUT GOD IS ALWAYS HIMSELF.[2]

Could Judas have gone back to Jesus? In the men's restroom of a restaurant in San Francisco Dr. Ray Anderson saw a note printed in block letters with a blue felt-tip pen across the top of the mirror:

JUDAS COME HOME—ALL IS FORGIVEN! The words caused Ray to stop.[3]

Could it be true? Would even Judas find forgiveness had he accepted the invitation and sought out the very One whom he had betrayed?

Why does Judas hurt himself instead of seeing a possibility of redemption? Because he knows Jesus only as a rabbi or teacher. When the knife of betrayal you have inflicted on another slashes your own heart, you need a Savior, not a teacher. You *need* a Healer greater than a mere human being. You need to know God's faithfulness. Judas never calls Jesus the Lord or Messiah, he only addresses Him as a rabbi. Judas kills himself for he does not know that Jesus is dying for *him*.

"What we think about God is the single most important thing in our spiritual journey."[4] What would Jesus have done for Judas if he had lived? Who do you trust Jesus to be for you?

Impressions of Jesus' Heart for Your Journey

My precious, I am not double-minded about you. I know all the propensities of your heart. Nevertheless, I remain faithful to you. Always choose to believe in My love and come home to Me. "Come now, let us settle the matter," says the LORD. "Though your sins are like scarlet, they shall be as white as snow; though they are red as crimson, they shall be like wool" (Isaiah 1:18).

Your Response

What stands out to you from today's reading and reflection? What is God saying to you? How do you want to respond to Him?

Your Lent companion,
Liena

Are You Willing to Go Where Jesus Goes?

Dear Friend,

A cross represents suffering of many kinds. Many crosses fall on us through the unpredictable storms of life, like illness and calamity. Some crosses are fashioned through poor life-choices. Then there are crosses we carry that God has never asked us to bear. We picked them up in our false humility as a result of misplaced responsibility. And finally, there are crosses we are privileged to bear with Jesus as we seek to spread the good news and expand God's kingdom.

Each and every cross calls for *prayerful discernment*. Some crosses need to be released, while others need to be embraced even harder. Which of these crosses are you carrying right now? I invite you to reflect on this as we witness Jesus' embracing of His own cross in today's passage.

Preparing to Reflect

I make myself comfortable in my chair and gently close my eyes or lower them to the floor. I sit straight and place both of my feet on the ground. I might turn my palms downward resting on my thighs. As I do this, I imagine Jesus kneeling before me with His open hands on my knees. I place my palms in Jesus' hands and look into His eyes. I relax my shoulders and allow any tension to drain from my body. I am here to be loved. Jesus has been waiting for me. He is all around me and before me. Nothing is missing.

Prayer

Loving Jesus, You have created me, chosen me, and called me to walk with You in this life and in the life everlasting. Claim my affections, mind, and will fully for Yourself today. Amen.

Story of the Day

So the soldiers took charge of Jesus. Carrying his own cross, he went out to the place of the Skull (which in Aramaic is called Golgotha) (John 19:16-17).

Entering the Scene

Jesus emerges from the judgment hall of Pilate to receive His cross. Working in the carpenter's shop, Jesus has laid His hands on wood almost daily, but this time it is different. Before He mastered lumber through His skills and control, but now He masters the tree by way of surrender. He welcomes, receives, and embraces His cross.

It is no coincidence that Jesus must bind Himself to the tree. By laying His heart and life on the timber, the Carpenter transforms the tree of death into the tree of life. The tree in Eden, through human choice, brought death; the tree of Calvary, through Christ's choice, brings life. The cross buds into the tree of life. Relish God's mystery and wisdom unfolding before your eyes!

Join Jesus' followers around the world in praise as you watch Jesus receiving His cross. "It is truly good, right, and salutary that we should at all times and in all places give thanks to You, holy Lord, almighty Father, everlasting God, through Jesus Christ, our Lord, who accomplished the salvation of mankind by the tree of the cross that, where death arose, there life also might rise again and that the serpent who overcame by the tree of the garden might likewise by the tree of the cross be overcome."[5]

Going Deeper

One of the things we love so much about God is that He always runs toward the danger, not away from it. The life of Jesus is not torn from Him, He *offers* it freely. Might He be asking the same of us? Might Jesus ask us to follow Him into places where we really would prefer not to go? He invites us into the life He lives, which is a life of love, sacrifice, and service. "If anyone would come after me, he must deny himself and take up his cross daily and follow me" (Luke 9:23 ESV).

My friend Miriam shared with me how her parents gave her the gift of seeing what it means to walk in Jesus' footsteps. This is what she said.

I had gone to visit my parents, and as soon as our initial greetings had been exchanged, my father said, "Your mother and I have some news to share." I followed them into the living room where they sat together on the couch holding hands, facing me. "We had an appointment with the neurologist this past week," my father began. "He informed us that your mother has Alzheimer's disease." My eyes darted to my mother's face. It was wreathed with a radiant smile. "We returned home and talked with Jesus about this. He told us that He is going into the valley of Alzheimer's Disease and wondered if we might be willing to accompany Him?" My father stopped and smiled at my mother. "We've never told Jesus 'no' before, and we agreed that is not in our hearts now to let Him go alone. We know it matters to Him when we show up, so we said 'yes.'"

My parents agreed to accompany Jesus to a place where no one wants to go. And over the next few years, they had many conversations with people who were suffering. My parents' awareness of the presence of Jesus in the lengthening shadows of memory loss was a great encouragement to those who found hope through their confident witness.

What am I willing to do for His sake? Am I willing to go where Jesus is going—even and especially when it is a place I would prefer to avoid? It is our opportunity to follow Jesus into absolute surrender. Our willingness to go is the deepest possible expression of intimacy to the One who has given all and withheld nothing.

"Learn to suffer in humility and in peace. Your deep self-love makes the cross too heavy to bear. Learn to suffer with simplicity and a heart full of love. If you do, you will not only be happy in spite of the cross but because of it. Love is pleased to suffer for the Well-Beloved. The cross which conforms you into His image is a consoling bond of love between you and Him."[6]

Impressions of Jesus' Heart for Your Journey

My child, when you find yourself beneath the yoke of the cross, be not quick to push it away. Resistance creates its own suffering, loneliness, and burden. Instead turn to Me. We will *discern* your cross together. We might lay it down, rest, welcome help, or carry it together. "And surely I am with you always, to the very end of the age" (Matthew 28:20).

Your Response

How do you find yourself after today's reflection and prayer? What word or words resonate in your heart? Is there any resistance you feel within you? Have an honest conversation with God in spoken or written prayer.

> *Be bound to Christ today and always,*
> *Your sister in Christ,*
> *Liena*

The Blessing of Interruptions

Dear Lent Pilgrim,

What is your first thought when you awake in the morning? It would not be surprising to have the agenda of the day be one of them. We proceed with rushing about our own business. And heaven forbid if we are interrupted in the flow of our day. Do you know that frustration?

But what truly are interruptions? What is God's design behind them? The story of Simon, a Cyrenian, challenges us to re-examine our daily interruptions in a new light. Let's take the opportunity to be with this man who just happens to be pursuing his business in Jerusalem when his own plans are frustrated and he is pulled into carrying a cross with Christ.

Preparing to Reflect

"The LORD is near to all who call on him, to all who call on Him in truth" (Psalm 145:18 ESV). I take a moment to reflect on movements in my spirit and soul. How do I find my heart today? What are the needs that whisper or even cry out for the touch and help of the living God? I choose to bring the truth to God in prayer.

Prayer

Lord, give me the double grace of knowing my true heart and Your heart. Connect me to Yourself in the shared fellowship of truth. Amen.

Story of the Day

A certain man from Cyrene, Simon, the father of Alexander and Rufus, was passing by on his way in from the country, and they forced him to carry the cross. (Mark 15:21).

Entering the Scene

The sun dawns upon the horizon and Simon awakes to another ordinary day. Today he is headed to Jerusalem to take care of some business. Hopefully all will go quickly and smoothly as desired.

As Simon approaches the city, the sound of a noisy mob meets his ear. "What is it?" he silently wonders. Simon pushes his way forward to catch a glimpse. Oh, another criminal labors to carry his cross. The felon is exhausted, dragging his feet, and tripping over the smallest of stones. The soldiers kick the criminal, frustrated by the delay. The offender does not have a drop of strength to carry on, but why should Simon care for this stranger deserving punishment?

The agenda of the day is waiting. Simon turns to go about his business when a soldier's heavy hand lays upon his shoulder. What does the soldier want? What does any of this have to do with him? How would you feel if you were Simon?

Confused and frightened, the Cyrenian is commanded to help the criminal carry his cross. Simon can't believe his bad luck. What are the chances that he would be dragged into this tragic procession? Humiliated and unaware that he is carrying the cross for humanity's and his own redemption, Simon climbs the hill of Calvary yoked with Christ.

Going Deeper

Simon is unaware, completely blind to what is actually happening. He is ashamed to be so closely associated with a condemned criminal, undeserving sinner, and Jew. Simon shifts the weight of the cross uncomfortably on his shoulder, the cross on which Christ will die for him. Simon has no sense that this embarrassing interruption is the greatest opportunity of his life. He has no awareness of the gift he is offering his own Savior.

Isn't this exactly what we encounter every day, God's work hidden in the interruptions of being asked to carry someone else's cross? Interruptions are God's stop signs that call us to pay attention, to be alert to what is happening.

Can you recall a time in your life when initially you were frustrated by the interruption of caring for someone else's need that turned out to be a *divine appointment* not just for them but also for you?

Interruptions are the norm in a chaplain's life. Daily I have the privilege of being called to carry a stranger's cross with them. When the pager goes off, there is no way of knowing who and what tragedy I will encounter. The truth is that I need the crosses I carry with my patients for my own sanctification as much as Simon needs the cross of Jesus for his own redemption. The crosses I carry with others give meaning and significance to my life. They grow in me the fruit of patience and compassion; they encourage me to eagerly seek the face of Christ in every encounter.

There is another side of this story. The soldier's choice to seize Simon is not incidental, but providential and illuminative of the Father's deepest will for Simon—and for all of us. Simon is pulled into Christ's suffering because the Father's intent is that *no one* should carry his cross alone. Jesus accepts Simon's reluctant help out of necessity, but in so doing, Jesus also shows us the way of humility. Acceptance of help is a *requirement* for those who want to be Jesus' disciples. "A man who claims to be self-sufficient and not to need any other man's help in hardship and suffering has no part in Christ. The pride which claims to be independent of human sympathy and practical help from others is un-Christian."[7]

Jesus also accepts John's willingness to care for His mother and the thief's compassion on the cross next to Him. He even accepts the provision of a garden tomb that was meant for someone else. *Jesus humbly and gratefully receives the help He needs.*

How is God calling you to be more Christ-like in accepting the help you need?

Impressions of Jesus's Heart for Your Journey

My dear one, I so appreciate you when you stop to address My direct need and My loneliness in people in whom I suffer. "Truly I tell you, whatever you did for one of the least of these brothers and sisters of mine, you did for me" (Matthew 25:40). Oh, what joy and fortitude awaits you as you put yourself aside for Me!

And let others serve Me in you through humbly accepting the help you need. Lay aside your pride so that others may love Me in you. I thank you.

Your Response

Ponder for a moment how God might help you to view your life's interruptions in this new light. And how do the above mentioned words "A man who claims to be self-sufficient has no part in Christ" speak to you? What is the prayer arising from your new awareness? Journal your thoughts to Him.

Take heart,
Your loving Lent friend.
Liena

_____
_____
_____
_____
_____
_____
_____
_____
_____
_____
_____
_____
_____
_____
_____
_____
_____
_____
_____
_____
_____
_____
_____
_____
_____

Will You Be with Jesus in Paradise?

Greetings,

The brilliance and creativity of God shines brightly through His redemptive work in our lives. There is nothing, absolutely nothing that God cannot redeem, use, or transform. He is always turning perils into riches. His greatest joy in reclamation. The Lord changes a sinner into a saint in a blink of an eye, like the criminal who hangs next to Jesus on the cross.

Where have you sensed God's joy of reclamation in your life? And where might the Lord want to perform His next miracle? Let's together approach the crosses of Jesus and the criminal.

Preparing to Reflect

I make myself comfortable for a conversation with the Lord. I might light a candle to represent His warm and loving presence with me. I remember that "Reality is God's home address."[8] What is the truth about my life and inner state right now? I bring that reality to my loving Father. He can only respond to what is true.

Prayer

Search me, God, and know my heart;
   test me and know my anxious thoughts.
See if there is any offensive way in me,
   and lead me in the way everlasting.
                Psalm 139:23-24

Story of the Day

One of the criminals who hung there hurled insults at him: "Aren't you the Christ? Save yourself and us!"

But the other criminal rebuked him. "Don't you fear God," he said, "since you are under the same sentence? We are punished justly, for we are getting what our deeds deserve. But this man has done nothing wrong."

Then he said, "Jesus remember me when you come into your kingdom."

Jesus answered him, "Truly I tell you, today you will be with me in paradise" (Luke 23:39-43).

Entering the Scene

Soon, very soon, Jesus will sit at the right hand of His Father, but right now He is crammed in between two criminals. At His birth Jesus had been enclosed by animals, at His death by two convicted men. At no point does Jesus remain aloof from the harsh realities of our world.

People mill around. The soldiers gamble noisily for the few personal items of the felons. Can you hear the mocking shouts and sneering challenges? "He saved others; let Him save Himself if He is God's Messiah, the Chosen One" (Luke 23:35). The crowd responds with coarse laughter and smirking.

Place yourself in this scene surrounded by a hostile crowd full of venomous hatred toward Jesus. What do you want to do? What do you want to say?

Before you get your chance, the sarcastic criminal shouts out: "Aren't you the Messiah? Save yourself and us!" (Luke 23:39). He finds a modicum of comfort by expressing his rage in taunting words. The other criminal remains silent as his conscience speaks louder with each breath. This felon watches till he can contain himself no longer.

This scene takes me back to the deathbed of some of my patients at the hospital. It's hard to believe, but at times, you find some family members arguing and bickering with each other while their loved one is seriously ill or dying. All I want to do at those times is to cry out, "Stop! This is a sacred moment!"

This is exactly what the contrite thief finally does. He challenges his fellow criminal, "Don't you fear God," he said, "since you are under the same sentence? We are punished justly, for we are getting what our deeds deserve. But this man has done nothing wrong" (Luke 23:40-41).

A pause sets in. A man who has lived his life exploiting others has placed himself between his blaspheming fellow convict and Jesus. Then his eyes meet those of Jesus, and the criminal speaks the most sincere words of his life, "Jesus, remember me when you come into your kingdom" (Luke 23:42).

Jesus' eyes lock with those of this earnest sinner and He utters a wonderful promise, "Truly I tell you, today you will be with me in paradise" (Luke 23:43).

Going Deeper

How graciously the Holy Spirit reveals Jesus' identity to the remorseful thief. This sinful man might know our Lord from previous encounters, because he addresses our Lord by His name, *Jesus*. He also knows that Jesus is innocent. Has he watched Jesus from a distance many times? Perhaps he has wanted to approach Christ before, but his shame tripped him up. Now they hang, crucified, mere feet apart.

Is the thief like many people who miss out on friendship with Jesus on this earth but find themselves desperate for salvation on their deathbeds? Have you known anyone like this man?

Ironically the criminal embraces Jesus at a time when it appears that our Lord is helpless to save anyone, including Himself! Jesus is "under every circumstance of weakness and disgrace. His enemies were triumphing over him. His friends had mostly forsaken him. Public opinion was unanimously against him. His very crucifixion was regarded as utterly inconsistent with his Messiahship."[9] Jesus' diminished condition appears to be an obstacle to anyone's faith. But is it? What if the Father is using this situation of shared weakness to reach the thief's heart? Nothing about Jesus intimidates the robber any longer. *Jesus' vulnerability and the thief's helplessness embrace each other.*

Reflect on your own journey for a moment. Have you ever felt that you need to be flawless to present the gospel to people around you? Have you ever believed that the salvation of your friends depends on how well you present the good news? We are reluctant to share our encounter with Jesus lest we express our faith in Him poorly and mess it up. But have you ever considered that your vulnerability might be God's tool? Notice how the Father uses *all* of the mental, emotional, and physical states of His Son in the Gospels to manifest Himself.

Contrary to every evidence of Jesus' weakness, the thief believes that Jesus can save His soul. Somehow, he sees through and beyond the sufferings of Jesus to the glory shortly to come. There is nothing—absolutely nothing—that the robber can do for himself now.

Look back at your life. Can you relate to him? When have you been "nailed to the cross?" Arthur Pink observes, "He could not walk in the paths of righteousness for there was a nail in either foot. He could not perform any good works for there was a nail through either hand. He could not turn over a new leaf and live a better life for he was dying."[10]

We only hear the thief's vulnerable request that he be remembered, that he be seen, that he not be forgotten and lost. Jesus does not reply: "It's too late. You've run out of time to get your life straightened out and undo the bad things you have done. Too late." Jesus also does not reply: "I'll keep that in mind as I review your case." What He says is, "Truly I tell you, today you will be with me in paradise" (Luke 23:43). How would you feel receiving this assurance from Jesus?

This thief would be the first of all humanity to follow Jesus into paradise! And this is possible because he simply asked! It is not the will of God that any of His little ones shall perish. "For it is by grace you have been saved, through faith—and this not from yourselves, it is the gift of God—not by works, so that no one can boast" (Ephesians 2:8-9).

Indeed, heaven and hell are not places far from us. They are near us. As near as both thieves were to Jesus on His cross. One entered paradise, the other did not. Everything depends on how we respond to Jesus. Which thief do you want to be?

Impressions of Jesus' Heart for Your Journey

My dear child, I am in My kingdom and I do remember you. I have more grace in My heart than you have sin in your past, present, and future. Come, follow Me into paradise. "I am the way and the truth and the life. No one comes to the Father except through me" (John 14:6). Welcome!

Your Response

How do you feel—surprised or encouraged—after being with Jesus and the two thieves? What do you want to say to Jesus? Journal your heart to Him.

May God hasten to help you,
Liena

Goodbye to Your Shame

Dear Friend,

Have you ever had one of those dreams where you were exposed in public? Psychologists say that as clothing is a means of concealment, this dream reflects feelings of shame and the fear of exposure. Let's be present with Jesus as He is stripped of dignity and publicly humiliated so that you will be released from your own shame.

Preparing to Reflect

The apostle Paul writes, "Three times I pleaded with the Lord to take it away from me. But he said to me, 'My grace is sufficient for you, for my power is made perfect in weakness.' Therefore I will boast all the more gladly about my weaknesses, so that Christ's power may rest on me" (2 Corinthians 12:8-9).

I pause to reflect on areas of *persistent* weakness in my own life. Where do I feel a particular sense of shame? I allow God to bring these painful areas to mind as I sit before Him in prayer.

Prayer

Heavenly Father, Lord Jesus Christ, indwelling Holy Spirit, I bring every part of who I am before You this day—the light and the darkness within me. Draw me into Your loving embrace and help me not only to know but to feel that I am Your beloved. Amen.

Story of the Day

Then the soldiers, when they had crucified Jesus, took His garments and made four parts, to each soldier a part, and also the tunic. Now the tunic

was without seam, woven from the top in one piece. They said therefore
among themselves, "Let us not tear it, but cast lots for it, whose it shall
be" that the Scripture might be fulfilled which says:
"They divided My garments among them,
And for My clothing they cast lots."
Therefore the soldiers did these things" (John 19:23-24 NKJV).

Entering the Scene

Where is the King of Glory? No one would recognize Him by now.
Jesus' head drops in shame upon His wounded chest. His bloody garments are stiff, adhering to His body, stuck into His bleeding wounds.
Fresh blood oozes through His clothes.

"Scorn has broken my heart and has left me helpless; I looked
for sympathy, but there was none, for comforters, but I found none"
(Psalm 69:20).

Who will behold Jesus with compassion? Not the soldiers. They
eye Him with hungry greed. A single thought possesses their minds,
"What can we get from this pitiful, disgusting sinner?" They tear Jesus'
clothing from His body with a swift and cruel move. Parts of His skin
is torn away. Jesus shrinks in an attempt to cover his exposed body.
How are you moved to behold Him or reach out to Him?

Jesus is stripped naked before the leering mob. The man they see
standing here is not the one that just a few hours ago was perfect,
strong, and admirable—in the prime of manhood. Jesus is bent over,
disfigured, weak with pain, humiliated by shame. Has your shame
ever been made public?

Even worse, Jesus' shame is exposed before His own mother, his
mother's sister, Mary the wife of Cleopas, Mary Magdalene, and John,
His beloved disciple. His disgrace is visible to the ones He loves the
most. Identify with Him for a moment.

Have parts of you, that you wished to keep secret, ever been
exposed to your loved ones? Come and understand what He did with
your shame on the cross, knowing He did it all for you.

Going Deeper

There is nowhere to hide. Every eye is fixed upon Jesus in His shattering humiliation. His experience is everyone's nightmare come true. Injury upon injury, indignity upon indignity, is heaped upon the unresisting Jesus as He is nailed to the cross. He is exhausted and grievously wounded. His heart fills with dismay as the hatred of His opponents flares into flame and stretches to consume Him.

Jesus looks down through swollen eyes to see the soldiers gamble for the beautiful, seamless tunic handwoven by His mother as a special gift. His eyes filling with tears, He gazes into His mother's upturned face. His heart breaks for her. They share a look of unspeakable sorrow.

Do we understand in this that Jesus knows exactly what it feels like to be shamed, beaten, disgraced, and maligned? Do we understand that He *chooses* to die on the cross in a strategic move to kill death and violence at its source? On the cross Jesus draws it *all* in so that in the future, there would be "no more death or mourning or crying or pain, for the old order of things has passed away" (Revelation 21:4).

The soldiers gambling for His clothing are oblivious to what is truly going on. The people passing by are oblivious. The mocking religious officials are oblivious. In what ways am *I* oblivious? In what ways am I blind to the fact that the source of my shame and embarrassment has been annihilated by the sacrifice of Jesus—that I am set free by the love of Jesus poured out for my salvation?

Late in the 14th century, Julian of Norwich was bedridden with a serious illness when she had an extended encounter with Jesus. The two of them engaged in conversation about the nature of sin, shame, and our salvation. She later wrote:

It is Christ's work to save us.
It is Christ's honor to help us.
It is Christ's will that we know this.

The cause why we are troubled is because of our ignorance of love. To this knowledge we are most blind; for some of us believe that God is all-powerful and can do anything. Some of us believe that God is all-wisdom and can do anything.

But we stop there. That God is all love and wishes to do every-thing—that we refuse to believe. It is this ignorance that most hinders those who love God.[11]

Jesus assured Julian: "All shall be well, and all shall be well, and all manner of things shall be well."[12]

How might Jesus be inviting you to rest in His love? How might He be inviting you to release your feelings of shame and, possibly, resentment to enter His peace? Healing begins with the knowledge that Jesus has removed the self-recrimination and rejection we fear. We are loved and accepted by the One whose acceptance *matters the most.*

Impressions of Jesus's Heart for Your Journey

My Beloved, the shame you felt or feel does not belong to you. I absorbed all your shame in My own shame on the cross. I bound up this humiliation and disgrace on the hill of Calvary and carried it with Me into the depths of hell. There I dealt it a deathblow. I suffered to gain freedom, esteem, and honor for *both* of us.

"Walk with me and work with me—watch how I do it. Learn the unforced rhythms of grace. I won't lay anything heavy or ill-fitting on you. Keep company with me and you'll learn to live freely and lightly" (Matthew 11:29-30 MSG).

Your Response

Ponder the fact that you are accepted. You are forgiven. Jesus assures you that all shall be well. Journal your response to His wonderful assurance.

With blessings,
Your Lent companion,
Liena

Lonely No More

Dear Fellow Traveler,

Do you remember a time in your life when you felt very lonely and wanted someone to care for you? When you lost a family member or a dear friend? Or when you felt utterly disconnected from the people closest to you? Perhaps you feel this loneliness right now. Journey with me as we witness Jesus providing for His mother's needs on His deathbed. Let yourself be curious about His provision for you in your circumstances.

Preparing to Reflect

God has been waiting with eagerness for this moment to connect with me and to speak to me. "It is not our prayer which moves the Lord Jesus. It is Jesus who moves us to pray. He knocks. Thereby he makes known his desire to come in to us. Our prayers are always a result of Jesus's knocking at our hearts' doors."[13] I take a few minutes to center myself in His presence. I might listen to quiet music or sing a song to Him to ready my heart for prayer.

Prayer

Father, prayer is first of all and foremost Your desire. Holy Spirit, give me Your grace to respond with heartfelt eagerness to my Father's longing. Free me from indifference, sluggishness, coldness of heart, and any other distractions. In Jesus' name, I pray. Amen.

Story of the Day

Near the cross of Jesus stood his mother, his mother's sister, Mary the

wife of Cleopas, and Mary Magdalene. When Jesus saw his mother
there, and the disciple whom he loved standing nearby, he said to
her, "Woman, here is your son," and to the disciple, "Here is your
mother." From that time on, this disciple took her into his home (John
19:25-27).

Entering the Scene

Mary stares up at her son. Everything but the figure of her battered
and bleeding son disappears from her view. The sword of sorrow
pierces right through Mary riveting her to His tree. Are Mary's
hands clutching His cross, the last tangible link between her and
her Son? Heaven knows how deeply she desires to snatch her innocent child out of this imminent danger and even to die in His place!
Wouldn't you feel this way if you were His mother?

It is unthinkable that "the hands that could raise the dead to
life with a touch, could heal the sick and give sight to the blind are
nailed to hard wood: unforgettable, stiffening in death. The feet
that blessed the delicate grass by their touch, that walked on the
swiftly moving waves of the storm at sea, are fastened down to the
rough trunk and held still. The eyes that could see into the depth of
the soul are darkened with the blindness of death. The tongue that
spoke the words of eternal love is swollen with thirst, and stiffened
in death. The heart of the man who is love is turning to a small, hard
stone that a man could hold in his hand!"[14]

John, Jesus' closest friend and disciple, weathers this absolute
nightmare *anchored in love*. Indeed, given the opportunity, he would
also exchange places with his Lord. If only he could reach Jesus to
offer Him some support. But now John has only one way to express
his love; he can offer comfort to Mary.

Their eyes fixed on the face of Jesus and joined by affliction, Mary
and John pour out the last drops of their strength to sweeten the cup
of the Savior's sorrow.

Jesus sees their travail, He feels the love they are pouring toward
Him. Mustering all that is within Him, Jesus lifts His head to whis-

per, "Woman, here is your son, "and to the disciple, "Here is your mother" (John 19:26-27).

Going Deeper

Mary stands in steady stillness, face upturned. Focused on the face of her son, she is determined to be strong for Jesus. "There she is: she does not crouch away, she does not faint, she does not even sink to the ground in her grief—she *stands*. What transcendent courage."[15] Strengthened from above, Mary conquers her fright and gives way to God's plan of Salvation. Her silence proclaims words that once she spoke aloud, "I am the Lord's servant . . . May your word to me be fulfilled" (Luke 1:38). Her presence confirms her ongoing surrender to the calling of her Son.

What is it like to be Mary? Sorrow has long since become her companion. She has watched her Son's reputation fall and rise throughout His ministry. Jesus has always been in the heat of both fame and surrounding danger. Mary has so desired to protect her Son, but many opportunities have eluded her. Now, despite His innocence, Jesus has been crucified.

As the blessed mother of Jesus, Mary holds a very unique place in God's plan of salvation. Her relationship to Jesus and the sorrow she carried uniquely enable her to identify with every woman whose child has been misunderstood and mistreated by the world. Mary weeps with every mother who cries "why" while watching illness and death steal her son or daughter. Mary grieves with every woman whose child's life appears to end in failure. And Mary is spiritually present to strengthen every mother whose fruit of the womb becomes a sacrifice of love for others.

Standing at the foot of the cross, Mary understands that she gave birth to Jesus for this hour. Have you ever have felt a bond with Mary in your own suffering? In faith I can envision how the Mother of God would bend close to embrace every mother huddling over her dead child at the hospital where I work.

What is Jesus' response to His mother's travail? Even at His darkest hour He thinks of her provision, asking John to assume His place as Mary's benefactor and protector.

Does Jesus remind you of anyone special in your life who thought of your wellbeing while on their deathbed? I am reminded of a dying patient whom I nurtured in her transition. She kept interchangeably crying out her daughter's and my name. Finally, it dawned on me what she wanted. "You want me to keep an eye on your daughter. Don't you? You want me to help her." With her final breath the mother whispered "yes" and died peacefully.

Isn't Jesus doing the same thing on His deathbed? Jesus releases His concern for His mother into John's hands, the friend whom He loves and trusts.

"When Christ said to him, 'Behold thy mother,' it was as though he had said, Let her be to thee as thine own mother: Let thy love for me be now manifested in thy tender regard for her."[16] When John agrees, a burden is lifted from Jesus' broken shoulders. But even more, Jesus gives John the most personal and precious inheritance of all—His dear mother.

How has God, by His loving design, given you family that is not from your own bloodline? Are you open to His provision and invitation to care for someone who needs a family to belong?

Impressions of Jesus's Heart for Your Journey

My child, I always think of you. You were on My mind when I walked this earth and left an inheritance of words and ministry to you who would accept it. Your face was before Me on My way to Calvary, strengthening Me to die for the one I love—you. And I continue to care for your needs. I desire to give you a mother, a father, sisters, brothers, and children in whom My Spirit dwells. "For whoever does the will of my Father in heaven is my brother and sister and mother" (Matthew 12:50). Open your heart to My family. Allow your love for Me to be expressed in tender regard for each other.

Your Response

What moves your heart in today's reflection? Allow yourself to rest in your loving conversation with Jesus. Feel free to express your heart in writing to Him.

With blessing,
Liena

Do You Need a Miracle in Your Life?

Hello again,

Today we will reflect on the miracle of forgiveness. Forgiveness sounds like a great idea until you are the one who has to do it. We all have wrestled with this issue. How can you forgive someone who has betrayed you? How can you offer forgiveness to a person bent on your destruction? How is Jesus able to forgive those responsible for His crucifixion? Come and hear Jesus' last words on the cross. Let Him teach and empower you.

Preparing to Reflect

I close my eyes for a moment and still my heart before the Lord. I recall the story of a sinful woman who knelt behind Jesus at His feet weeping. Kissing and wiping His feet with her hair, she poured perfume on them. I imagine myself being that person and Jesus defending me before the other disciples, "Therefore, I tell you, her sins, which are many, have been forgiven—for she loved much. But he who is forgiven little loves little" (Luke 7:47ESV). I ask myself: what are *the specific* instances of God's forgiveness that have enabled me to love much?

Prayer

Jesus, I ask Your forgiveness to transform my heart into a living flame of love for You and all who have sinned against me. Amen.

Story of the Day

When they came to the place called the Skull, there they crucified him there, along with the criminals–one on his right, the other on his left. Jesus said, "Father, forgive them, for they do not know what they are doing" (Luke 23:33-34 ESV).

Entering the Scene

Together, an exhausted Jesus and Simon of Cyrene slowly climb the hill of Calvary. Simon is relieved to finally toss Jesus' cross on the ground and flee the scene.

The merciless soldiers push the feeble Jesus down onto His death cradle—the cross. The first time they crucified someone, their hearts might have been moved by its brutality, but by now they are hardened, detached, and cold to Jesus' loving stare. The soldiers pound the nails through Jesus palms and feet, calloused to His cries of torment.

Jesus holds Himself to the cross with His will of love for you, me, and them. Yes, even now Christ could throw over each one these soldiers and walk away victorious in human eyes. If so "people would have feared Him for all time, but they would not have loved Him. But in His physical weakness as a human being, in His struggle to the cross and on the cross, Christ identified Himself with all the weak and sinful of the ages to come who would be healed by His wounds: 'And I, if I be lifted up, will draw all men to me.'"[17]

The soldiers raise Jesus' cross. The tree sways back and forward stretching Jesus' wounds until it is dropped into the hole.

The soldier's duty is done—one of many this single week. Bored, the soldiers pass their time gambling over the victim's few possessions while waiting for their death to come. It's not a rarity to hear curse words from the crosses behind them. In sharp contrast, Jesus' powerful and loving words pierce through their dullness. "Father, forgive them, for they do not know what they are doing" (Luke 23:34). Is Jesus already drawing all people to Himself?

Place yourself there. What is the soldiers' response to His words?

Going Deeper

All through His adult life, His enemies attempted to destroy Jesus.

When, finally, their evil resolve is fulfilled, Jesus offers a plea for God to pardon those responsible for His death.

As a human being Jesus has established a *practice* of being merciful and forgiving even when it hurts. He has practiced it over and over again until offering pardon has become a way of life. When the pain is fiercest, when His anguish is the sharpest, words of forgiveness slip from His swollen lips, "Father, forgive them, for they do not know what they are doing" (Luke 23:34).

What don't they know? They don't know that they are crucifying their Maker. They don't know that they are crucifying the One who loves them most. They don't know that Jesus is letting them crucify Him to secure their salvation! They don't know that the Evil One sits on the throne of their hardened hearts and laughs about their ignorance and ruin.

Take a look at the people who have ever needed or need your forgiveness now. Meditate on the following question for a while. "What does she or he not know?" Can Christ-like mercy and prayer arise in your heart?

If you want to see a guaranteed miracle in your life, forgive. When our *agape* unites with God's *agape* over a hurt, *always* a miracle is birthed. Frederica Mathewes-Green shares a very touching story about Pastor Richard Wurmbrand who comes from Eastern Europe. He was in a Communist prison when he witnessed a victim, Fr. Iscu, and his torturer ending up in the same prison cell because the perpetrator had fallen out of Communist favor. The Communist officer was dying and pled Pastor Wurmbrand to pray for him.

He kept saying, "I can't die, I have committed such terrible crimes." Fr. Iscu, on the other side, had been listening. After a while he called for two other prisoners to help him. Leaning on them, he slowly and painfully made his way to the officer's bed. He sat on the bedside and reached out to caress the miserable man's head. "I will never forget this gesture," said Pastor Wurmbrand. "I watched a murdered man caressing his murderer!" Fr. Iscu told the officer, "You are young, you did not know what you were doing. I love you with all my heart." Then he said, "If I who am a sinner can love you so much, imagine Christ, who is Love Incarnate, how much He loves you! And all the Christians who you have tortured, know that they forgive you, they love you, and Christ loves you. He wishes you to be saved much more than you wish to be saved. You wonder if your sins can be forgiven. He wishes to forgive your sins more than you wish your sins to be forgiven. He desires for you to be in heaven much more than your wish to be in heaven with Him. He is Love. You only need to turn to Him and repent." With that, the officer choked out the words of his confession with tears, the priest, the one who he had tortured, spoke the words of God's forgiveness.[18]

In His Sermon on the Mount, Jesus tells us to pay forward the grace we have received. "Pray for those who spitefully use you and persecute you" (Matthew 5:44 NKJV). Jesus says it, then He does it to break the endless cycle of revenge.

Michael Crosby declares, "The crucifixions can end with us. The scapegoating need find no more victims or perpetrators in us. It all begins when we too can say 'Father, forgive them, for they do not know what they are doing.'"[19]

To be clear, forgiveness is not to be confused with the vulnerability of enabling abuse in our lives. Sin has to be named and confronted. "Permitting abuse could make you an enabler and partner in that sin. Forgive the past, but make wise decisions about the present and future."[20] We are called to both: forgive always and discern any situation well.

To whom is Jesus asking you to extend pardon?

Impressions of Jesus' Heart for Your Journey

My child, every time you hurt I hurt. I desire to heal and strengthen you. Even more I want to give you My vision to see every situation in My light. Don't strive to forgive in your own feeble strength, but let Me forgive *in* and *through* you. "My grace is sufficient for you, for my power is made perfect in weakness" (2 Corinthians 12:9). Your willingness joined with My love will birth the next miracle.

Your Response

How do you find yourself after today's mediation and prayer? What is the Holy Spirit praying in you? Give voice to His prayer.

With love,
Liena

The Fifth Week of Lent

I Thirst

Dear Child of God,

Imagine yourself in the desert. Your throat is parched. You can think of nothing other than liquid. You would plead and give anything for a drink of water.

Is this thirst also true in your spiritual life? Has there ever been a time when your inner spiritual dryness seemed too much to bear? Has your prayer life ever dried up and God seemed distant?

Saint Teresa of Calcutta, recognized by our generation as a living saint, struggled in this way. "My soul remains in deep darkness and desolation. I don't complain—let Him do with me whatever He wants."[1] Surrendering anew, Mother Teresa sacrificed willingly the consolation of a felt union with Jesus for the challenge of living by pure faith. In so doing, she followed in the footsteps of her Lord who willingly entered the darkness for the sake of our salvation.

Preparing to Reflect

"Blessed are those who hunger and thirst for righteousness, for they shall be filled" (Matthew 5:6 NKJV). As I prepare to reflect on the barren, wilderness places of the spiritual path, I settle into my prayer chair and close my eyes. I think of a time, perhaps even now, when I hungered and thirsted in my relationship with God. Conversation was difficult. I didn't know what to say. Could today be a day of new revelation? Can I allow Him to refresh me?

Prayer

Dear heavenly Father, Lord Jesus Christ, indwelling Holy Spirit, I lift my hands, palms open, and offer You these desolate feelings. Receive them, holy Trinity, as my most difficult and precious gift. May I, in turn, receive the gift that You so desire to give me in this quiet hour. I am yours. Show me what You will. Amen.

Story of the Day

Later, knowing that everything had now been finished, and so that Scripture would be fulfilled, Jesus said, "I am thirsty." A jar of wine vinegar was there, so they soaked a sponge in it, put the sponge on a stalk of the hyssop plant, and lifted it to Jesus' lips (John 19:28-29).

Entering the Scene

Jesus has been on the cross for several hours by now. His shoulders, out of joint, burn in agony. Our Lord can't pull Himself up any longer to take a breath. With His head hanging, Jesus draws shallow and short inhales. His lips are parched. The breeze blowing past makes Jesus' mouth even dryer. His tongue has dried up like a wooden twig in the wind. If He could, He would mutter,

> I am poured out like water,
>   and all my bones are out of joint. My heart has turned to wax;
>   it has melted within me.
> My mouth is dried up like a potsherd,
>   and my tongue sticks to the roof of my mouth;
>   you lay me in the dust of death.
>   Psalm 22:14-15

The prophecy in Psalm 69:21 is fulfilled, "They put gall in my food and gave me vinegar for my thirst." In our place Jesus drinks the last drop from the cup of wrath poured out (Matthew 26:39).

Now, when it's finished, is He thirsting not only for water but also *our* consoling love? Could it be that Jesus thirsts for *you* and *me*? Is He expressing His longing that each of us would follow Him into a renewed intimacy with the Father, Son, and Spirit? Is Jesus anxious that some would choose not to follow? That for them, His death would be in vain? Could it be?

Going Deeper

Saint Teresa of Calcutta meditated deeply on the thirst of Jesus. Her heartrending experience of suffering humanity was, she discovered, intimately shared with Jesus. He was the one weeping in the night over our broken world. Interior darkness was her privileged way of entering into the mystery of the cross of Christ. Jesus gave her a letter to pass along to us.

Do you thirst for love?

"Come to Me all you who thirst ... " (John 7:37). I will satisfy you and fill you.

Do you thirst to be loved?

I love you more than you can imagine ... to the point of dying on a cross for you.

I THIRST FOR YOU. Yes, that is the only way to even begin to describe My love for you.

I THIRST FOR YOU. I thirst to love you and to be loved by you . So precious are you to Me that I THIRST FOR YOU. Come to Me, and I will fill your heart and heal your wounds. I will make you a new creation and give you peace even in your trials.

I THIRST FOR YOU.

You must never doubt My mercy, My desire to forgive, My longing to bless you and live My life in you, and that I accept you no matter what you have done.

I THIRST FOR YOU.

If you feel of little value before the eyes of the world, it doesn't matter. There is no one that interests me

in the whole world more than you.

I THIRST FOR YOU.

Open up to Me, come to Me, thirst for Me, give me your life. I will prove to you how important you are for My Heart.

Don't you realize that My Father already has a perfect plan to transform your life, beginning from this moment? Trust in Me. Ask Me every day to enter and take charge of your life and I will. I promise you before My Father in Heaven that I will work miracles in your life. Why would I do this?

Because I THIRST FOR YOU.[2]

Recall how Jesus asks the Samaritan woman for a drink of water in the Gospel of John (4:7), "Will you give me a drink?" They both satisfy each other's thirst and drink from each other's hearts.

Are you drinking deeply from the cup of the salvation Jesus places in your hands? Are you letting Him feel the satisfaction of your soothing love? "I thirst"—do these words echo in your soul?

Impressions of Jesus' Heart for Your Journey

Dear one, whenever you open the door of your heart, whenever you come close enough, you will know that no matter what you have done, I love you for your own sake. "I stand at the door and knock" (Revelation 3:20)—the door of your heart. Open to Me, for I thirst for you.

Your Response

Ponder the thirst of Jesus. What do you feel as you read the letter Jesus asked Mother Teresa to give you? What is the prayer raising from this awareness? Journal your response to Jesus.

Your grateful Lent friend,
Liena

Don't Waste Your Cross!

Dear Reader,

Why? Why? You probably have heard this question on the lips of those who suffer. Most likely your own heart has uttered this question. Have you, like Jesus, cried aloud, "My God why have you forsaken me?" Have you felt abandoned by God?

Take heart and stand at the cross of Jesus. What might be the true spirit of His cry for mercy? Today let His *why* speak into your *whys*.

Preparing to Reflect

As I prepare to pray, I might make a cup of tea or coffee to help me relax and really slow down. I envision opening the door of my heart to welcome God's Word.

> He wakens me morning by morning,
>   wakens my ear to listen like one being taught.
> The Sovereign LORD has opened my ears;
> I have not been rebellious,
>   I have not turned away.
>
> Isaiah 50:4-5

I lean close to Him and listen.

Prayer

Loving God, "Your word is a lamp to my feet and a light to my path" (Psalm 119:105 ESV). Shed Your light on my life's circumstances, oh Lord. May I see myself and my life in Your light today. Amen.

Story of the Day

Now from the sixth hour until the ninth hour there was darkness over all the land. And about the ninth hour Jesus cried out with a loud voice, saying, "Eli, Eloi, lama sabachthani?"that is, "My God, My God, why have You forsaken Me?"(Matthew 27:45-46 NKJV).

Jesus called out with a loud voice, "Father, into Your hands I commit My spirit." Having said this, He breathed His last (Luke 23:46 NKJV).

Entering the Scene

The soldiers strain to lift the cross with Jesus' body attached and drop it in the hole. His bloodshot and startled eyes hunt for mercy. The weight of Jesus' body tears the pierced wounds. Open your senses to this horrifying scene. What do you hear? What do you see? What do you smell?

The pain contracts Jesus' body in relentless waves of agony till no one can look into His eyes. The heart of the Father and the Holy Spirit sink into the deepest of sorrows, like the sun setting on the sea. Suddenly a veil of darkness descends, quenching the brightness of midday. Imagine being here, on the Hill of Calvary, in the midst of a complete blackout. What's that like?

The heavy blackness whispers of death and impending judgment, mirroring the eclipse of the human soul. All activity halts. Conversations stop in mid-sentence. "What's happening?" everyone wonders. An uneasy stillness creeps into every corner and every space. Is this the end of the world?

And then, a wounded wail shreds the pitch-black darkness, "My God, my God, why have You forsaken Me?" (Matthew 27:46 NKJV). Hear the echo travel across the streets of Jerusalem, petitioning every heart, "Have you forsaken your God?"

Going Deeper

What do we hear in Jesus' cry? What is the mystery in His agonized question, "Why have You forsaken Me?"

Jesus has always addressed His Father in the familiar household manner, "Abba"—daddy. It is only now that we hear the word *Elohim* on Jesus' lips. Jesus brings us back to the creation of the world, "In the beginning *Elohim* created heaven and earth" (Genesis 1:1 NOG). *El* means "mighty; strong", while the ending, *him*, is plural, indicating more than one person. We come to know these persons later in Scripture as Father, Son, and Holy Spirit.

Is Jesus' cry prompting us to recollect that all members of the Trinity are committed to our deliverance? That the saving work of the cross of Jesus was conceived in close partnership with God the Father and the Holy Spirit? As Zechariah declares at the birth of his son, John the Baptist, Jesus comes "because of the tender mercy of our God" (Luke 1:78).

Some believe that God is cruel and harsh, while Jesus is loving and sacrificial. But this is not so. On the cross, the entire Trinity pays the price. The Cross is by far the Father, Son, and Spirit's most costly undertaking. In redeeming us, They let our sin temporally lacerate Their perfect communion. Jesus's cry is the agony of being torn apart from the Father and the Spirit by the weight of our sin. The mystery is deep: in His separation Jesus eliminates forever our separation from the Trinity. "It is finished" (John 19:30). Jesus consummates His love for you and me on the cross. *This is the ultimate God's love affair.* The Lover dies His bride's death. The door to everlasting life and union with God swings wide open.

Now, together with Paul, we can shout, "I am convinced that nothing can ever separate us from God's love. Neither death nor life, neither angels nor demons, neither our fears for today nor our worries about tomorrow—not even the powers of hell can separate us from God's love. No power in the sky above or in the earth below—indeed, nothing in all creation will ever be able to separate us from the love of God that is revealed in Christ Jesus our Lord" (Romams 8:38-39 NLT).

Paul is saying, "Don't let your suffering create the illusion of abandonment." The most dangerous sin and offense against God is our belief that somehow *Elohim* is against us. This deep delusion results in self-induced misery. So many of our troubles and sins toward ourselves and others, are rooted in our forgetfulness that we are loved.

How might you undertake the sacred battle against the lie of God's indifference?

Impressions of Jesus' Heart for Your Journey

My child, I used My cross to consummate My love for you. Don't waste your cross! Don't allow bitterness, resentfulness, or doubt to allure you away from My embrace. "Above all guard your heart, for it is the wellspring of life" (Proverbs 4:23).

Your Response

How do you find yourself after today's prayer time? Where do you feel a challenge? Where do you hear an invitation from Jesus? Talk with Him about your feelings.

Peace to you,
Liena

_____
_____
_____
_____
_____
_____
_____
_____
_____
_____
_____
_____
_____
_____
_____
_____
_____
_____
_____
_____
_____
_____
_____
_____
_____
_____
_____

Are You Expectant with Life?

Christ's Beloved,

At times we find ourselves being shut out from our own lives behind a heavy stone of suffering. Do you recall ever feeling internally "deceased" and separated from God and life itself? Today's passage invites us to be with Jesus who is lying still and lifeless in His tomb waiting for His resurrection. I invite you to explore with Jesus this mystery as you wait for your own soul's rebirth.

Preparing to Reflect

In Isaiah 55:10-12 find the image of God's Word and grace falling like rain upon the hardened and dead spots of my life.

I settle into my prayer chair and locate myself in this passage. I imagine being drizzled upon as I read the following words:

As the rain and the snow
   come down from heaven,
and do not return to it
   without watering the earth
and making it bud and flourish,
   so that it yields seed for the sower and bread for the eater, so is my word that goes out from my mouth:
   It will not return to me empty,
but will accomplish what I desire
   and achieve the purpose for which I sent it.
 You will go out in joy
   and be led forth in peace;
the mountains and hills

will burst into song before you,
and all the trees of the field
will clap their hands.

Can I allow myself to believe that today's Scripture is God's promise to me—that God longs to refresh me and give me hope?

Prayer

Lord, I surrender to You as a seed surrenders to the soil and waits. I rely on You Holy Spirit, my Living Water, to penetrate to the hard shell of my soul and call forth life from within me. I wait, expectant before You. Amen.

Story of the Day

Later, Joseph of Arimathea asked Pilate for the body of Jesus. Now Joseph was a disciple of Jesus, but secretly because he feared the Jews. With Pilate's permission, he came and took the body away. He was accompanied by Nicodemus, the man who earlier had visited Jesus at night. Nicodemus brought a mixture of myrrh and aloes, about seventy-five pounds. Taking Jesus' body, the two of them wrapped it, with the spices, in strips of linen. This was in accordance with Jewish burial customs. At the place where Jesus was crucified, there was a garden, and in the garden a new tomb, in which no one had ever been laid. Because it was the Jewish day of Preparation and since the tomb was nearby, they laid Jesus there. (John 19:38-42).

Entering the Scene

Night is falling. Every heart loving Jesus is emptied out, crushed, bone-weary. People wander without purpose, dazed by grief. The disciples, disoriented and afraid, flee to hide in the cloak of the night. How would you feel if you were one of Jesus' followers? The One you knew to be God's Messiah is impossibly dead. Perhaps you will be next.

To everyone's surprise, in the most extreme hour of despair, two of Jesus' secret disciples, Joseph from Arimathea and Nicodemus, appear on the scene. In the dark hour when fear has put Jesus' professing disciples to flight, the Father moves the hearts of two hidden followers to exhibit utmost boldness in taking ownership of Jesus' body. The Father moves the last to be the first to provide dignity for His Son. "Without specific instructions, a victim of crucifixion would be removed by the Roman soldiers on duty and hauled to a nearby valley called "Himnon" where it would be unceremoniously "dumped" into the pit located there with the rest of the city's trash, then sprinkled with sulphur powder and left to burn and rot."[3] Joseph and Nicodemus joined together to give Jesus an honorable burial. The other disciples almost certainly would have undervalued and taken little notice of these two saints. But now Joseph and Nicodemus risk their own reputations and lives to care for their Lord.

They tenderly pull the nails from Jesus' hands and feet and receive the Lord's body onto their shoulders. They lift Him down from the cross and carefully lay Jesus on the ground. The men bend down, sprinkling a generous amount of spice over Jesus' grievous wounds. They move quickly for the Sabbath is approaching when all work must cease.

Do Joseph and Nicodemus speak? Do they exchange words or glances? What is this brotherhood like? How does it feel to finally express their affection and care for Jesus in public? I invite you to help them wrap Jesus' body in the finest of linen and carry it to the tomb.

The tomb is in a garden, a symbol of life in the presence of death. Look around. What do you see and smell here? Jesus' burial and His birth bear striking similarities: they are like two ends of the same thread tied together in a circle. When Jesus was born, He was laid in a stranger's manger; and now, upon His death, Jesus is laid in a borrowed tomb. He owned no earthly possessions, yet the Father provided so beautifully for His needs. What is the promise for us in this?

Finally, you and the two disciples lay Jesus' body in the empty tomb. Can you choose to remain with Jesus inside the grave when the disciples roll the stone to seal the entrance? Now it is just you and the Lord. Lifeless silence settles in; it is cold. What is it like for you to be with Jesus' body in the tomb?

Going Deeper

Does staying there with Jesus remind you of a season in your life when you felt bound in burial clothes through illness, depression, or a dark night of the soul?

These experiences can feel much like the night of Jesus' burial, lifeless and hopeless. Yet there has not been another night in all of human history so ready to burst with life. This night is full of promise, expectancy, and the Father's excitement to raise His Son from the dead. As the sorrows of the world deepen, the hope of heaven expands. The seed of Christ's body is about to break through the shell of its confinement, defeating the powers of hell and death. "Very truly I tell you, unless a kernel of wheat falls to the ground and dies, it remains only a single seed. But if it dies, it produces many seeds" (John 12:24). Is your spiritual, emotional, or physical seed about to break into life?

My friend Miriam shares a beautiful story about her friend Andrea who was able, through God's grace, to perceive her own dying body as a seed ready to burst with new life. The following is what Andrea shared with Miriam.

> One evening several months ago, I was very upset. I asked Jesus why He did not cure me. Why, if He had it within His ability to heal, did He allow the cancer to spread? Jesus moved close until I could feel His arms surround me, and He whispered, "Andrea, you know what this is. You understand germination. Don't look too close at the seed; look deeper to see the beauty waiting to be revealed."
>
> In a flash of insight, I saw what Jesus meant. When I earned my master's degree in Horticulture, I learned all about seeds and growth. Did you know that seeds are amazingly complex? A single seed, like a mustard seed, for example, has a remarkable nutritional profile, including vitamins A, B6, phosphorus, potassium, sodium, and zinc, just to name a few—all enclosed

in a tiny seed less than two millimeters in diameter! The full potential of the plant is contained within that tiny seed. Jesus explained that I was never meant to remain a seed, enclosed and protected. My seed coat *had* to be cracked to allow the embryo of my soul to grow. Jesus said that just looking at the seed of my soul, it was impossible to know what was hidden inside, that I wouldn't know until it burst into blossom. But that when it did, it would take my breath away.

That's what Jesus told me. So I have been applying what I know about seeds and germination to the growth of my soul. In both cases, God alone can bring the growth. As gardeners, we cooperate by assuring that the surrounding soil is full of the proper nutrients and has enough water. So what kind of soil does a soul need to thrive and grow? I have identified the core disciplines of Jesus as providing the essential nutrients, and like-minded companions who water my soul by increasing my ability to cooperate with the Holy Spirit in the germination of my soul. Despite everything, I am feeling very optimistic.

Two weeks later, Andrea's "seed coat" split open, allowing the sprout of her resurrected soul to push up and break through to new life. Her final words to Miriam were: "Responding to God's transforming work requires bravery—we must be brave. We must allow God to find the crack and pry it open. We must make spaces to pray, to deepen our trust in God and accept the help of trusted friends, because God is at work. It may be hard to imagine, but God is doing something beautiful in us that will burst forth into life."

"For this slight momentary affliction is preparing us for an eternal weight of glory beyond all measure, because we look not at what can be seen but at what cannot be seen; for what can be seen is temporary, but what cannot be seen is eternal" (2 Corinthians 4:17-18 NRSV).

Impressions of Jesus's Heart for Your Journey

My dear sister and brother, wait with Me. Rest; be at peace. Trust in our Father's work. The hour of your resurrection is also approaching. Our Father is giving you the grace of experiencing Him beyond your own terms and boundaries. In your darkness He is claiming you completely for Himself, purifying and alluring your will and desire for Him alone. Rest easy with an expectant heart! "Wait for the LORD; be strong and take heart and wait for the LORD" (Psalm 27:14).

Your Response

How do you find yourself after this meditation? What is your response to the invitation to wait with Jesus? Express your heart in writing or journaling.

With many blessings,
Liena

Jesus' Last Mission Trip

Dear Lent Pilgrim,

Have you ever wondered what Jesus was doing in His Spirit while His body was waiting resurrection in the cold tomb? He did not rest. No! He went on His last mission trip to proclaim the Good News to the captives in the world of the dead. Even between His death and resurrection Jesus did ministry. Let's go with Him to proclaim the words of salvation to all!

Preparing to Reflect

As I am about to embark on the story of this day, I lay down all my distractions and gently instruct my heart to take a break from my daily worries. I let myself ponder Jesus' courage to descend into the world of the dead. Even darkness is as light to Him. I let myself soak in His victory, radiance, and omnipresence.

> Where can I go from your Spirit?
> Where can I flee from your presence?
> If I go up to the heavens, you are there;
> if I make my bed in the depths, you are there.
> If I rise on the wings of the dawn,
> if I settle on the far side of the sea,
> even there your hand will guide me,
> your right hand will hold me fast.
> If I say, "Surely the darkness will hide me
> and the light become night around me,"
> even the darkness will not be dark to you;
> the night will shine like the day,
> for darkness is as light to you.
> Psalm 139:7-12

Prayer

I thank You, Jesus, that even the dimmest darkness is like a light to You. Give me Your heart of courage to enter every and any situation with Your victorious light and confidence. Amen.

Story of the Day

For Christ died for sins once and for all, the righteous for the unrighteous, to bring you to God. He was put to death in the body but made alive by the Spirit, through whom also he went and preached to the spirits in prison.... (1 Peter 3:18-20).

Entering the Scene

Who can stop our Lord? No one. Jesus goes where only He can go—into the adobe of the dead, Hades in Greek and Sheol in Hebrew. Jesus does what only He can do—break open the prison doors to lead the captives out.

Imagine descending with Jesus into the world of the dead. What is the atmosphere like? The captives bow their heads in fear, shame, sadness, and eternal despair, knowing they have no hope to escape. The prison guards have every right to keep them.

Jesus arrives with a completely different demeanor. He comes as the One who is ready to release His enemy's hostages after paying the price on the cross. How do the spirits in Sheol react to Jesus' presence—the presence of the Savior? How would you describe the intensity of their surprise and relief after ages of suffering? When Jesus starts to proclaim the Good News to them, what response does He get? Did fear leave the prisoners and enter their guards? Can you imagine the first worship services breaking out in the Hades, the territory of the enemy?

Yes, Jesus, descends into Sheol to bring the gospel message of salvation to complete fulfilment. Without descending into Hades, His victory would be partial, leaving a territory unclaimed and unliberated. This is the last mission trip Jesus takes in His messianic work before

His splendid resurrection and reign. Our Lord's will is to offer His redemption to all men of all times and in all places, even those who died before He was born. Jesus is the Savior "who wants all people to be saved and to come to a knowledge of the truth" (1 Timothy 2:4). Jesus' plunge into Sheol is the ultimate depth of His care for all souls. How does Jesus' comprehensive love inspire and move you?

Going Deeper

So many Christian believers around the world confess their faith through the Apostles' Creed every Sunday, including the following words about Jesus, "He descended to the dead." But it is not often that we stop to reflect upon the meaning of Jesus' last mission trip.

Just this last Easter season, I was working at the hospital the weekend after Jesus' crucifixion. I noticed that the lady who delivers the food was very reflective. I approached her and inquired about her well-being. She looked at me and shared, "I am thinking about Jesus being in Hades. What was it like for Him to go to that prison for the love of all of those lost souls? For us it is a peaceful Saturday, but how about Him?" After this conversation, for the first time in my life, I specifically gave thanks for the fairness of God's love toward all people of all ages. Indeed, His love is so thorough, without an error, and all-inclusive. His gift of salvation is offered to all only to be claimed.

Jesus' descent into Sheol takes my heart on a pilgrimage to reflect upon those times I have seen Him go to "the end of world" for us. I know a Christian sister who before her conversion was sold as a prostitute to the Japanese mafia. There was no way she could free herself or escape. One afternoon she was sleeping on a mat in her room. She happened to be by herself which had never been the case before; many girls share the same room. Suddenly a big earthquake shook her awake and she heard a voice say, "Get up and leave." Even as a non-believer she recognized God's voice. Jesus came for her in an earthquake. She escaped her prison through the confusion caused by the earthquake and became a believer.

How has Jesus shaken the doors of your "hades prison" and set you free? Do you believe that to be with you Jesus has done and given everything?

Impressions of Jesus' Heart for Your Journey

There is no place or state out of My reach. Trust that even your darkest darkness is as a light to me. Your darkness does not intimidate Me for "I am the Light of the world. So if you follow me, you won't be stumbling through the darkness, for living light will flood your path" (John 8:12 TLB).

Your Response

How do you find your heart after today's reflection? What encourages and comforts you? What does Jesus want you to understand? Talk to Him as your closest friend.

With love,
Liena

Resurrected Now!

My Friend,

He is risen. Risen indeed! Just recently my colleague left me a note on my desk, quoting John Paul II, "Do not abandon yourselves to despair. We are the Easter people and hallelujah is our song."[4]

These words challenge me to examine my life and ask myself the following questions, "How does my life reflect Jesus' resurrection?" "Does the world hear me singing hallelujah?" Please join me today as we reflect on these questions together.

Preparing to Reflect

I pause for a moment and appreciate God's life pulsating through me and in every creature around me. I recall Isaiah's vision of seraphim praising God,

And they were calling to one another:

> "Holy, holy, holy is the Lord Almighty;
> the whole earth is full of his glory."
> Isaiah 6:3

How is God's presence and glory evident to me in this moment?

Prayer

May none of God's wonderful works keep silent,
night or morning.
Bright stars,
high mountains,
the depths of the seas,

sources of rushing rivers;
may all these break into song
as we sing to Father, Son and Holy Spirit.
May all the angels in the heavens reply
Amen! Amen! Amen!
Power, praise, honor, eternal glory to God,
the only giver of grace.
Amen! Amen! Amen!

Anonymous Christian author[5]

Story of the Day

When the Sabbath was over, Mary Magdalene, Mary the mother of James, and Salome bought spices so that they might go to anoint Jesus' body. Very early on the first day of the week, just after sunrise, they were on their way to the tomb and they asked each other, "Who will roll the stone away from the entrance of the tomb?" (Mark 16:1-3).

There was a violent earthquake, for an angel of the Lord came down from heaven and, going to the tomb, rolled back the stone and sat on it. His appearance was like lightning, and his clothes were white as snow. The guards were so afraid of him that they shook and became like dead men. . . .

Some of the guards went into the city and reported to the chief priests everything that had happened. When the chief priests had met with the elders and devised a plan, they gave the soldiers a large sum of money, telling them, "You are to say, 'His disciples came during the night and stole him away while we were asleep.' If this report gets to the governor, we will satisfy him and keep you out of trouble." So the soldiers took the money and did as they were instructed. And this story has been widely circulated among the Jews to this very day (Matthew 28:2-4, 11-15).

Entering the Scene

Finally, the dawn breaks the darkness of the dreadful and sleepless night. Jesus' women disciples have been impatiently waiting through-out the slow moving hours of Sabbath in obedience to Sabbath rest.

Now they can rush to the tomb of their rabbi. Rise and hurry with them. Let yourself experience the mood of this morning.

Deceased bodies were normally anointed with oil before the burial. Since Jesus died just before the Sabbath, this anointing has been postponed. Love and care compels Mary Magdalene and the other Mary to charge forward. Jesus' body has to be protected from the rapid decomposition in the Mediterranean heat!

Both followers know that it is logically impossible to remove the stone blocking the entrance to Jesus' grave. The disk-shaped stone is huge and sealed, watched by Roman soldiers. They worry but go anyway to move "this mountain" in faith.

The guards, sluggish and bored, sit around fighting their exhaustion till the fiercest tremor shakes the earth. Have you ever been in an earthquake? The watchmen and women stumble around terrified, trying to catch themselves from falling. The stones split open like a celebration fanfare. Hear the cracks of falling gravel mixed with human cries.

A blinding light shoots down from heaven. An angel of the Lord descends to roll back the stone with effortless ease. He proceeds to sit on it like a king on his throne. What is the expression on this angel's face? How does heaven celebrate Jesus' resurrection?

The nearly paralyzed guards stagger into the city to report the missing Jesus to the chief priests. How is the news delivered and received? As a witness, what do you see and hear?

Instead of repenting and acknowledging Jesus' resurrection, the religious leaders conspire with the guards to lie to the people. "And this story has been widely circulated among the Jews to this very day" (Matthew 28:15).

Going Deeper

No lies can hide Him. Jesus is risen indeed! And our journey is to be like our Lord's in every single way, including our bodily resurrection. In Matthew 27:52-53 we have a foreshadowing illustration of what will happen to all of us, "The tombs broke open. The bodies of many holy people who had died were raised to life. They came out of the tombs after Jesus' resurrection and went into the holy city and appeared to many people."

We are created to share His entire nature and glory, and to be fully restored in soul, spirit, and *body*. Jesus who walked out of His tomb on Easter morning is a *prototype* of what will happen to us. "The risen Christ is the standing icon of humanity in its full and final destiny. He is the pledge and guarantee of what God will do with all our crucifixions. At last we can meaningfully live with hope. It is no longer an absurd or tragic universe. *Our hurts now become the home for our greatest hopes.*"[6]

Resurrection is *simultaneously* our future and present reality. The Lord makes the same power, the Holy Spirit who resurrected Jesus from the dead, available to us even today.

We do not have to wait for death for our transformation to commence! When Jesus rose from the dead, God's new creation began. Forty days later, on Pentecost Sunday, the Holy Spirit arrived as promised to equip the followers of Jesus to live as resurrection people, demonstrating through their lives and actions the restored life that Jesus makes possible. In this very moment, the heartbeat of the Holy Spirit who rose Jesus from the dead beats in our spirit, transforming us from the inside out.

Every day we are coming alive to the reality of our post-Easter world, but some days we need a gentle reminder of our important role in God's reclamation project. We need someone to say, "Wake up! You have important work to do today! Do something *kind* that makes God's new creation visible for someone else!" Robert Fulghum tells a beautiful story of Professor Dr. Papaderos illustrating the way we can live as an Easter people.

When I was a small child, during the war, we were very poor and we lived in a remote village. One day, on the road, I found the broken pieces of a mirror. A German motorcycle had been wrecked in that place. I tried to find all the pieces and put them together, but it was not possible, so I kept only the largest piece.

And by scratching it on a stone, I made it round. I began to play with it as a toy and became fascinated by the fact that I could reflect light into dark places where the sun would never shine—in deep holes and crevices and dark closets. It became a game for me to get light into the most inaccessible places I could find.

As I became a man, I grew to understand that this was not just a child's game but a metaphor for what I might do with my life. I came to understand that I am not the light or the source of light. But light—truth, understanding, knowledge, faith—is there, and it will only shine in many dark places if I reflect it.[7]

How is God calling you to reflect God's light into the dark places of our world?

Impressions of Jesus' Heart for Your Journey

My beloved, "I am the resurrection and the life. The one who believes in me will live, even though they die; and whoever lives by believing in me will never die. Do you believe this?" (John 11:25-26).

Your Response

Take a minute to reflect on Jesus' question and today's message. Talk to Him as a friend would talk to a friend.

Let us sing together Hallelujah,
Liena

The Great Race

Dear Lent Pilgrim,

There is something so fascinating about the race—the courage, endurance, and devotion it takes. Saint Paul says, "I have fought the good fight, I have finished the race, I have kept the faith" (2 Timothy 4:7). Is this something you would like to be able to say? Today's gospel story portrays two of Jesus' disciples running a race. What can we learn from them?

Preparing to Reflect

Prayer is a place of encouragement. The Lord desires me to come to Him so that He can encourage me for "the race" I am running in my life. I pause and cease from my daily activities to be reassured. I center down and listen for a few minutes. What words of encouragement is the Holy Spirit conveying to my spirit today?

Prayer

"Father, Your grace has no measure and it was graciously extended to me the hour I first believed and started my spiritual race. You not only prepared the way but You also run alongside me and enable me to throw off those things that hinder or weigh me down. You've given me an enduring spirit to stay on course during the desirable and undesirable starts of new chapters in my life. It's not the one who runs the swiftest, nor the one who runs for a day, but it's the one who endures to the end that will be saved. I want to be among that number, and by Your grace, I will receive the eternal rewards that come to those who finish well. And then I start the next chapter that never has an ending; that of living in heaven and praising You for all eternity. I can hardly wait. Amen."[8]

Story of the Day

Now on the first day of the week Mary Magdalene came to the tomb early, while it was still dark, and saw that the stone had been taken away from the tomb. So she ran and went to Simon Peter and the other disciple, the one whom Jesus loved, and said to them, "They have taken the Lord out of the tomb, and we do not know where they have laid him." So Peter went out with the other disciple, and they were going toward the tomb. Both of them were running together, but the other disciple outran Peter and reached the tomb first. And stooping to look in, he saw the linen cloths lying there, but he did not go in. Then Simon Peter came, following him, and went into the tomb. He saw the linen cloths lying there, and the face cloth, which had been on Jesus' head, not lying with the linen cloths but folded up in a place by itself. Then the other disciple, who had reached the tomb first, also went in, and he saw and believed; for as yet they did not understand the Scripture, that he must rise from the dead (John 20:1-9 ESV).

Entering the Scene

Mary Magdalene runs till she almost collapses. Panting, she swings the door open to the disciples' dwelling. "They have taken the Lord out of the tomb, and we do not know where they have laid him" (John 20:2 ESV). How do you envision her in this moment?

Startled, Peter and the other disciple bolt out the door for the empty tomb. Mary follows. The beloved disciple outruns Peter, but he freezes at the entrance of the tomb. He only views the linens from a distance. What holds him back?

Peter being last becomes first to witness the absence of Jesus' body. He sees the *sidon* or burial shroud, and the *soudarion* or head cloth that passed under Jesus' chin and was tied on the top of His head to keep his mouth from falling open. Notice the first piece is still laying on the ledge of the tomb where his body had laid, but the second is mindfully folded. No thief would bother about these details.

Stay with Peter and the other disciple in the tomb for a while. What is the feeling in this empty burial chamber?

Sadly, the disciples truly believe that Jesus has been stolen. They turn and walk away "for as yet they did not understand the Scripture, that he must rise from the dead" (John 20:9 ESV). The disciples believe that they have lost Jesus twice: on the cross and, now, from the tomb.

Going Deeper

I have always been fascinated about the race of Peter and Jesus' beloved disciple. It reminds me of all the "races" we run in our lives. We pursue visions, callings, relationships, emotional healing, and spiritual transformation. Many times, we are almost there, but then we stop like Peter's friend at the entrance to the tomb. As a result, we are not the first to claim the reward of a resurrection miracle—whatever it might be. Like the disciple whom Jesus loves, we are "outrun" by something else. We halt because of our fears, exhaustion, "cold feet," or discouragement.

What is "the race" you are running right now in your life? Where are you in your "race"? If you are stopping by the entrance to "the resurrection tomb," what holds you back from going all the way?

The folded linens also captivate me. Apparently, Jesus or the angel has taken the time to fold graveclothes after the resurrection. Jesus has left a sign of His presence and fingerprints for His disciples, but they fail to notice. There is order, not chaos, in His tomb.

The Lord invites us to always look for "the folded linens," the sign of His presence and intentionality in every situation that feels grave-like. If there is a painful situation in your life right now, where do you notice "the folded linen cloth"—the hints of His resurrection and hope for you?

Pain and suffering have a tendency to turn us inward and make us self- (and problem) centered. It becomes difficult to truly see others and the signs of resurrection that surround us. The disciples are so upset with Jesus being stolen that they miss the evidence of His resurrection. The prophet Isaiah says, "You have seen many things, but you pay no attention; your ears are open, but you do not listen" (Isaiah 42:20). Paying attention includes lifting our eyes from ourselves and taking a closer look at the entire picture. In what ways is the Holy Spirit prompting you to use a wider lens as you examine your life?

Impressions of Jesus' Heart for Your Journey

Run the race I have set before you with confidence in My presence. "Be strong and courageous. Do not be frightened, and do not be dismayed, for the LORD your God is with you wherever you go" (Joshua 1:9 ESV).

Your Response

What movements do you notice in your heart today? Talk to the Lord about them.

Take heart,
Liena

Called to Belong

Dear Reader,

We all have experienced the power of being called by name, especially those moments when we hear the sound of our name being delivered on the wings of love and affection. It can make your day, and it can soothe away our sadness. In today's passage Jesus opens Mary's eyes to the resurrection miracle through calling her by name.

Saying a person's name with love is ministry in itself. How are you and I called to this practice in more deliberate and intentional ways? Let's learn from Jesus.

Preparing to Reflect

There are many passages in the Scriptures talking about God calling me by name. I take a brief moment to still myself before the Lord and say my name slowly and lovingly several times. Then I visualize the Lord saying my name with utter tenderness and adoration, "Do not fear, for I have redeemed you; I have summoned you by name; you are mine" (Isaiah 43:1).

Prayer

My loving God, You say to me, "Behold, I have graven thee upon the palms of my hands" (Isaiah 49:16 KJV). Yes, my Lord, I behold the beauty of being claimed. I give thanks and receive Your affection. Amen.

Story of the Day

Then the disciples went back to where they were staying.

Now Mary stood outside the tomb crying. As she wept, she bent over to look into the tomb and saw two angels in white, seated where Jesus' body had been, one at the head and the other at the foot.

They asked her, "Woman, why are you crying?"

"They have taken my Lord away," she said, "and I don't know where they have put him." At this, she turned around and saw Jesus standing there, but she did not realize that it was Jesus.

He asked her, "Woman, why are you crying? Who is it you are looking for?"

Thinking he was the gardener, she said, "Sir, if you have carried him away, tell me where you have put him, and I will get him."

Jesus said to her, "Mary."

She turned toward him and cried out in Aramaic, "Rabboni!" (which means "Teacher").

Jesus said, "Do not hold on to me, for I have not yet ascended to the Father. Go instead to my brothers and tell them, 'I am ascending to my Father and your Father, to my God and your God.'"

Mary Magdalene went to the disciples with the news: "I have seen the Lord!" And she told them that he had said these things to her (John 20:10-18).

Entering the Scene

"Blessed are those who mourn, for they will be comforted" (Matthew 5:4). Blessed is Mary for she takes time to mourn, to be true to her love for Jesus.

In disbelief and grief that Jesus is taken, Mary leans into the tomb one last time just to make sure. Her tear-filled eyes meet two men in dazzling white. She mistakes angels for two ordinary men. They ask an almos ignorant question, "Why are you crying?"

Mary's tenderness for Jesus spills over and she emphasizes that "my Lord" is taken away instead of "the Lord," and "I" don't know where He is instead of "we." She turns around in grief and meets yet another stranger asking the same question. In hopes that this man is a gardener, Mary pleads for His help. The wound of loss is so deep that it does not allow any possibility of life in Mary's mind. She can't see Jesus till He *intentionally* calls her by name, "Mary."

None of us can perceive Jesus to be the risen Christ *until* He calls us intimately by our name. Mary's conversion, as does ours, starts right at this point.

If you were Mary, what would you do? Collapse at Jesus' feet? Embrace Him to never let Him go? With the greatest difficulty yet joy Mary turns around to run to her brothers in Christ to announce the good news.

Going Deeper

Mary *lingers*. This is the precise reason she meets the risen Christ. She does not rush away from His absence as the other disciples do.

Lingering is crucial in our Christian walk, just that extra mile that Jesus asks us to walk, "And whoever will compel thee to go one mile, go with him two" (Matthew 5:41 DARBY).

I have experienced this many times in my prayer life. In plenty of occasions I have been tempted to stop praying and get up when the Lord seems to be absent. But, oh, how I have been surprised by the Presence, if I choose to *linger* just for a few extra minutes longer than I want! Have you experienced anything similar in your prayer life?

This dynamic has been true so many times in my chaplaincy work as well. One day I was making rounds and entered a man's room. He was somewhat withdrawn, and I noticed fear and sadness in his face. The conversation started slowly and did not seem to go much deeper. I could have left, but I chose to linger just for a few extra minutes and ask a couple more questions. To my surprise the conversation started to open up. I noticed an accent. I myself speak with an accent. I thought he was from the East coast. Then I asked, "Where are you from?"

He answered, "From Latvia."

"So am I!" I replied in surprise.

Tears started to pour down his face. Shortly after he confessed, "I have been running from God all my life. My sister called me from

Latvia yesterday and said, 'Brother, I am praying that God would send someone to comfort you.' I cannot deny the existence of God any longer."

We cried, we laughed, and we prayed together. The discomfort of lingering paid off in the most beautiful way. It gave Jesus the opportunity to call this man by name.

Have there been any unexpected turns in your lingering experiences?

When Jesus calls us by name, He recognizes, honors, loves, and claims us in one breath. Have you ever experienced this in your spirit?

Romans 9:28 (MSG) describes God's utter intentionality. "God doesn't count us; he calls us by name. Arithmetic is not his focus." When Jesus says, "Mary," He means, "Do not fear, for I have redeemed you; I have summoned you by name; you are mine" (Isaiah 43:1). This is *how* He *always* says your name! Behold the beauty of the Lord as He beholds and treasures you.

Impressions of Jesus' Heart for Your Journey

When you call Me by name, you seek My presence. When I call you by your name, I offer you a belonging. This is written about Me, the Good Shepherd, "he calls his own sheep by name and leads them out" (John 10:3). Come and follow Me in the belonging of love.

Your Response

How can you become more intentional about learning people's names and addressing them with deliberate love? Talk to Jesus about this opportunity.

May every blessing be yours,
Liena

Discovering Resurrection

Returning for You

God's Child,

Do you remember playing hide and seek and the thrill of being found even though you hid? Deep in our hearts we all desire to be worthy of someone discovering and treasuring us. And even coming back for us. Today's Scripture passage speaks to this need. Let's journey together.

Preparing to Reflect

Being present and aware of God's presence is a spiritual discipline acquired through faithful practice. I might start my reflection today by reviewing the last twenty-four hours. Where did I feel God's presence hidden under daily realities? I give thanks for those specific moments of awareness. Did I notice resisting the Lord in any way and withdrawing or turning away from Him, others, and my own true heart? I confess my dismissiveness. I continue by asking for grace to be fully awake to His presence going forward.

Prayer

Loving God, give me the gift of tracing Your hand over my life-span and every day. Awaken me to Your presence. Amen.

Story of the Day

On the evening of that first day of the week, when the disciples were together, with the doors locked for fear of the Jewish leaders, Jesus came and stood among them and said, "Peace be with you!" After he said this, he showed them his hands and side. The disciples were overjoyed when they saw the Lord.

Again Jesus said, "Peace be with you! As the Father has sent me, I am sending you." And with that he breathed on them and said, "Receive the Holy Spirit. If you forgive anyone's sins, their sins are forgiven; if you do not forgive them, they are not forgiven."

Now Thomas (also known as Didymus), one of the Twelve, was not with the disciples when Jesus came. So the other disciples told him, "We have seen the Lord!"

But he said to them, "Unless I see the nail marks in his hands and put my finger where the nails were, and put my hand into his side, I will not believe."

A week later his disciples were in the house again, and Thomas was with them. Though the doors were locked, Jesus came and stood among them and said, "Peace be with you!" Then he said to Thomas, "Put your finger here; see my hands. Reach out your hand and put it into my side. Stop doubting and believe."

Thomas said to him, "My Lord and my God!"

Then Jesus told him, "Because you have seen me, you have believed; blessed are those who have not seen and yet have believed."

Jesus performed many other signs in the presence of his disciples, which are not recorded in this book. But these are written that you may believe that Jesus is the Messiah, the Son of God, and that by believing you may have life in his name (John 20:19-31).

Entering the Scene

After Jesus' arrest and death, the disciples hide, concerned that they, too, might be persecuted. They gather behind locked doors to strategize how to escape Jerusalem and move on with their lives. Place yourself among them. What conversations do you hear?

Jesus startles them and interrupts their plans with a sudden appearance. What expressions do you read on the disciples' faces? An outburst of joy follows the initial shock. Are they laughing, praising God, dancing, touching Jesus, or flooding the Lord with questions? Everyone, except Thomas, witnesses Jesus alive and well! Don't you wonder where he is?

When Thomas returns, he finds the others all animated with the news of the resurrected Jesus! He is taken aback. Imagine being Thomas. Would you wonder, "*If* it is true that Jesus is alive, why didn't He wait to come when I was here? Why *them* and not me?" Have you ever felt like that? Have you wondered, "Why does God make His presence known to others and not to me?"

Thomas feels isolated and irritated. Finally, he shuts the others up by exclaiming, "Unless I see the nail marks in his hands and put my finger where the nails were, and put my hand into his side, I will not believe" (John 20:25). That is effective; no one talks with Thomas about it after that. But note, Thomas stays put and waits for an entire week. He stays with the fellowship *even though* he does not agree! What would you do in his place? Would you stay? Or you would you go? Imagine the conversations swirling around Thomas for that entire week.

When Jesus returns, He walks straight over to Thomas. He extends His wounded hands and says, "Put your finger here!" Jesus invites the pragmatist to review the evidence and *believe*. In awe Thomas follows Jesus' invitation. Then Jesus pulls open His robe to reveal the wound in His side and continues, "Reach out your hand and put it into my side" (John 20:27). Thomas slides his entire hand into Jesus' wounded side feeling the warmth of Jesus' flesh. Be Thomas for the moment and experience the intimacy of this connection. What do you feel?

Going Deeper

Jesus could say many retributive things to His disciples when He sees them for the first time after His resurrection. After all, they deserted, denied, and left Him alone to suffer. But He does not. He offers a greeting of peace in exchange for their fears. Instead of saying "Shame on you," Jesus says, "Peace be with you!" (John 20:19). Jesus puts the past to rest completely.

God has no need to remind us of our failures; He operates within complete forgiveness and extends the gift of a blessed future. Jesus breathes the Holy Spirit over His friends like God did once for Adam in the garden of Eden. This moment marks the rebirth of the new Adam in His disciples.

When Jesus returns the second time, He comes back *specifically* for Thomas, the one lost "sheep." Can you sense Jesus' desire? He hears Thomas in His absence and comes back to address Thomas' need and grief-devastated heart. Jesus perceives Thomas' "hanging" on the cliff of unbelief and returns to pull his disciple back into resurrected life.

The literal Greek translation of Jesus' address to Thomas is "become not unbelieving." *Just when* Thomas thought to be excluded, he becomes included beyond his imagination. Only he, the one who questioned, gets to place his hand in Jesus' side.

Pragmatic, practical Thomas is completely flabbergasted! He hardly knows what to say. Overcome with emotion, doubter-turned-believer breathes out a prayer: "My Lord and my God!" (John 20:28). The precise Greek wording is, "the Lord of me and the God of me." Thomas' prayer expresses *surrender*—the Lord of me—and *worship*—the God of me. Thomas' prayer keeps us alert to the Jesus who exceeds all our expectations and who stretches our imagination of what is possible in our life with Him.

How has God "come back" just for you and surprised you when you thought He had excluded you from a blessing?

And what does it mean for Jesus to have His wounds be validated by a human touch?

The scene of exposed wounds is very familiar to me as a chaplain. People uncover and show me their wounds often. It's important for their healing process that someone compassionately looks at their wounds, sees what they are, and validates their experience. It's equally true for our physical and emotional healing. Is there anything in you that aches for validation?

The gesture of Jesus' return just for Thomas affirms His eagerness to work with pragmatic people and also His delight in those who are more intuitive, "blessed are those who have not seen and yet have believed" (John 20:29). We are *all* are the object of His desire.

Impressions of Jesus' Heart for Your Journey

I would leave the hundred sheep, just to come back for you. If you would be the only person on the earth, I still would die for you. Do you believe this? "Blessed are those who have not seen and yet have believed" (John 20:29).

Your Response

How has Jesus' interaction with Thomas moved your heart today? Journal and pray your experience.

May the Lord keep you from all harm,
Liena

_____
_____
_____
_____
_____
_____
_____
_____
_____
_____
_____
_____
_____
_____
_____
_____
_____
_____
_____
_____
_____
_____
_____
_____
_____
_____
_____

Jesus, the Listening Stranger

Dear Reader,

Often people who experience grief keep it to themselves. Words fail to express the depth of the loss they have experienced. So, they fall into silence. They withdraw. Have you been there?

On the afternoon of Easter, two of Jesus' disciples experience a huge and unexpected shock. However, they chose to talk about it among themselves as they walk to the village of Emmaus until Jesus comes alongside of them.

How can you let Jesus accompany you in your moments of loss and despair?

Preparing to Reflect

"Authentic prayer is opening to God's gracious presence with all that we are, with what Scripture summarizes as our whole heart, soul, and mind (Matthew 22:37). Therefore prayer is more a way of *being* than an isolated act of doing. Prayer is aimed at our deepest problem: our tendency to forget our liberating connectedness with God. When this happens we become lost in a sense of ultimate separateness. From this narrow outside-of-God place rise our worst fears, cravings, restlessness, and personal and social sinfulness."[1]

I remember that I am here to connect and remember my belonging to and within God. I begin my prayer time by breathing deeply for a few minutes. With each inhale I think, "God, may all that is from You come to me." With each exhale I think, "God, free my life from all that is not of You."

Prayer

Lord, help me to remember that in you I live, move, and have my being. (Acts 17:28) Give me confidence in your faithful presence. Amen.

Story of the Day

Now that same day two of them were going to a village called Emmaus, about seven miles from Jerusalem. They were talking with each other about everything that had happened. As they talked and discussed these things with each other, Jesus himself came up and walked along with them; but they were kept from recognizing him.

He asked them, "What are you discussing together as you walk along?"

They stood still, their faces downcast. One of them, named Cleopas, asked him, "Are you the only one visiting Jerusalem who does not know the things that have happened there in these days?"

"What things?" he asked.

"About Jesus of Nazareth," they replied. "He was a prophet, powerful in word and deed before God and all the people. The chief priests and our rulers handed him over to be sentenced to death, and they crucified him; but we had hoped that he was the one who was going to redeem Israel. And what is more, it is the third day since all this took place. In addition, some of our women amazed us. They went to the tomb early this morning but didn't find his body. They came and told us that they had seen a vision of angels, who said he was alive. Then some of our companions went to the tomb and found it just as the women had said, but they did not see Jesus."

He said to them, "How foolish you are, and how slow to believe all that the prophets have spoken! Did not the Messiah have to suffer these things and then enter his glory?" And beginning with Moses and all the Prophets, he explained to them what was said in all the Scriptures concerning himself (Luke 24:13-27).

Entering the Scene

Imagine being Cleopas walking the seven mile road from Jerusalem to your home in Emmaus. Your steps are lead-heavy from all the grief, stress, and disappointment absorbed in your body. You are in a deep conversation with your fellow companion about the tragic end of following this rabbi, Jesus. "How could something feel so true and end up in utter disaster?" you ask each other. So many days and so much energy totally wasted.

Then, suddenly, a stranger strolls up to you and asks to join you with a question, "What are you discussing with each other while you walk along?" This question is bold, bordering on intrusive. You stand there downcast for a minute, washed with grief and sadness all over again. You are faced with a quick decision: to brush off the outsider or to welcome him into your no-holds-barred conversation and perhaps listen to what he has to say. There are many Passover pilgrims heading home; he probably is one of them. You choose to be open, curious, and vulnerable, not knowing that this split-second decision will change your life forever.

Does this encounter, welcoming a stranger into one's vulnerable space, remind you of life-transforming occasions in your life?

Soon you discover that your companion-stranger is completely oblivious. How could he have missed the top news: the disturbing events surrounding Jesus in Jerusalem? You almost can't stand his ignorance and blurt out, "Are you the only stranger in Jerusalem who does not know the things that have taken place there in these days?" The stranger's answer is shocking, "What things?"

But something about this man's presence and innocence summons you to share what happened to Jesus. Before you realize, you have poured out all your pain, disillusionment, and disappointment.

What follows next, surprises you even more. The stranger names the condition of your heart and starts explaining the Scriptures concerning Jesus in the most enticing and enlightening way. Soon an overpowering and increasing sensation of fire consumes your heart. An increasing knowing sweeps through all your senses. "It's true! It's true!"

Going Deeper

One of the truths we discover in the story of the Emmaus Road is this: spiritual transformation does not occur in isolation. God brings people into our lives who help us to find perspective and discern God's presence in our current circumstances. This is not something we can discover on our own.

Now when we feel off-balance, the temptation for most of us is to withdraw and isolate. Had the two companions made this choice, had they kept it buried all inside, had they failed to include Jesus in their conversation, they would have remained stuck. End of story.

But they do not isolate; they do not lock down. They do not refuse Jesus or try to put a good face on it. They welcome the stranger into their story, and He turns out to be a messenger sent from God. This encounter changes everything.

The disciples' choice to walk together and talk about all the things that had happened to them was, in some ways, fairly radical. They could have decided that what they had been through was so personal, so traumatic and so confounding that they didn't want to talk about it until they had gotten a handle on it. Or they could have chosen to walk together but avoided talking about what was really going on, chatting about anything else but *that*. But no. While the experiences of the weekend were still fresh and raw, unvarnished and unresolved, they chose to walk together and talk with each other about all these things that had happened. The reason this was such a crucial choice was that there is something about the willingness to walk together and speak honestly about the fundamental issues of our lives that causes Jesus himself to come near.[2]

And when Jesus comes near, the first thing He does is *listen*!

There are different ways of listening. We can listen with one ear tuned to the news report on television, we can listen while glancing around the coffee shop to see if there is anyone else we know, or we can listen while scanning through emails on our phone. It is easy to listen with divided attention.

Conversations that matter are different. Jesus gives the two disciples His *undivided* heart and attention. Before He says anything, Jesus listens carefully. He is a good chaplain to these two men on the road to Emmaus.

In my ministry I have learned that listening in its deepest sense is a ministry of presence and deliverance. Jesus' loving, compassionate, and attentive presence pulls open the inner prison gates of His companions and all the terrorizing fear and pain are freed to be appraised in God's light. Sacred listening always frees people from concealed darkness.

Do you remember a time when someone listened to you so well that you were delivered from your internal prison? And how are you being called to *listening deliverance* creating healing in other people's lives?

Jesus shapes His response from what He hears. This attentiveness results in a transforming encounter. The words He chooses touches His listeners deeply. The story Jesus tells invites His companions to trust God *even now, even in this.*

The Emmaus Road story invites us—you and me—to honestly consider:

How comfortable am I with the life God has given to me? How satisfied am I with my current circumstances? Is it possible that God is in this—even *this? Am I able to discuss this openly with a trusted few?*

Impressions of Jesus' Heart for Your Journey

My friend, I have come to you as a stranger so many times. "I needed clothes and you clothed me, I was sick and you looked after me, I was in prison and you came to visit me" (Matthew 25:36). Thank you. Look for Me and you will see Me.

Your Response

How does the Emmaus story invite you to approach your encounters with strangers? Talk to Jesus about this.

With love,
Liena

Persevering in Seeking

Dear Fellow Seeker,

I remember Christian teacher Graham Cooke sharing that any new circumstance, including suffering, gives an opportunity for God to be for us who He has not been for us yet. Any new challenge gives us the opportunity to experience God in a new way. We witness this reality in the progressive revelation of Jesus to His disciples on the road to Emmaus.

Who does Jesus want to be for you in your present circumstance? Ask this question while diving into today's story.

Preparing to Reflect

Contemplation is "our direct, loving, receptive, trusting presence for God. This attention includes the desire to be present through and beyond our images, thoughts, and feelings."[3] I just sit quietly for a few minutes and offer my deep desire to hear from Him today.

Prayer

Infinite God of boundless and new revelation, let Your Word and heart be revealed to me. Let me comprehend with all the saints what is the breadth, the length, the depth, and height of Your love for me (Ephesians 3:18). Amen.

The Text of the Day

As they approached the village to which they were going, Jesus continued on as if he were going farther. But they urged him strongly, "Stay with us, for it is nearly evening; the day is almost over." So he went in to stay with them.

When he was at the table with them, he took bread, gave thanks, broke it and began to give it to them. Then their eyes were opened and they recognized him, and he disappeared from their sight. They asked each other, "Were not our hearts burning within us while he talked with us on the road and opened the Scriptures to us?"

They got up and returned at once to Jerusalem. There they found the Eleven and those with them, assembled together and saying, "It is true! The Lord has risen and has appeared to Simon." Then the two told what had happened on the way, and how Jesus was recognized by them when he broke the bread (Luke 24:28-35).

Entering the Scene

Many miles vanish unnoticed in the heat of the disciples' conversation with Jesus. Jesus' explanation of the Scriptures sets Cleopas and his friend's hearts on fire. Connect with them by remembering a time in your life when a message, an inspiration, or an internal realization was so powerful that you sensed your heart being ablaze. Take note, the disciples' sight is sealed, but their hearts are burning. They journey by faith, compelled by an inner movement. Before they know it, all three men have reached the little village of Emmaus.

As Cleopas and his companion near their destination, they don't want their conversation with the stranger to end. Jesus gives them the impression that He is going on farther. Why? He wants His disciples *to exercise obedience to their inner fire!* And He wants to be invited. The disciples in obedience to God's command to welcome strangers beg Jesus to stay with them.

When they are about to share supper, a dramatic change takes place. Jesus takes the initiative of reaching for the bread. Place yourself among them. What do you notice? Where is your attention drawn to?

Suddenly the disciples' eyes are fastened to the movement of the stranger's hands. They have seen this before! Scales fall from their eyes, and their inner fire is confirmed in an instant. It's Jesus! Before the disciples can say or do anything, Jesus vanishes. It's like He is conveying, "*Enough* has been given for you to be my witnesses!"

The disciples don't waste any time but hasten back to Jerusalem to tell others of their experience. They have to share their burning hearts with others, "his word is in my heart like a fire, a fire shut up in my bones. I am weary of holding it in; indeed, I cannot (Jeremiah 20:9). Join them! What kind of thoughts accompany your steps?

Going Deeper

The walk to Emmaus is about two powerful ways of transformation: being deeply listened to and learning how to listen well. The two disciples are on the way home because they did not listen well in Jerusalem. They did not take seriously the testimony of the women, and they did not listen carefully to Peter and John's report (John 20:1-8). Jesus joins them on the road to give them a second chance of *paying attention.* Jesus gives them the gift of *time, patience,* and *good questions.* The Lord reviews the Scriptures with them once again and gifts them with the opportunity of not dismissing the inner fire they are feeling in their hearts.

My most significant lifetime repentance has involved being a dismissive listener to the nudging of the Holy Spirit during a particular event that led to a very painful outcome. I rationalized myself in a decision versus listened to His still voice. Since then, my life has been devoted to learning discernment and being faithful to "the fires" in my heart.

What has been your journey of following your inner fire and guidance? What are your obstacles? How loyal do you feel to your own heart?

Jesus has given me other chances to become a good listener. He does the same for His disciples on the way to Emmaus and also for you.

This time around Cleopas and his friend don't ignore their *burning hearts* and *attraction* to this stranger. They listen. They follow their internal pull and beg Jesus to stay with them, which leads to an amazing progression of revelation.

As soon as Jesus breaks the bread, scales fall from the disciples' eyes and they see in full.

The entire Emmaus Road experience was really an exercise in discerning Christ's presence-on the road, in conversation, in Scriptures, during the meal. The issue never was whether Christ was present in all these moments, for he surely was! The issue was whether the disciples had the capacity to recognize him, and *that* was something that developed by God's grace, over time, as they shared the journey. Their ability to discern the presence of Christ progressed throughout the story: first they saw him as a stranger, then as a traveling companion, then as a teacher, then as a guest, then as a host, and finally as their Messiah and resurrected Lord.[4]

As we persevere in our seeking, Jesus promises to reveal Himself to us. How has your own revelation of Jesus deepened during the last five years of your life?

Impressions of Jesus' Heart for Your Journey

I want to be more for you than I am for you now. Let Me, invite Me, be curious and open. "Trust in the LORD with all your heart and lean not on your own understanding; in all your ways submit to him, and he will make your paths straight" (Proverbs 3:5-6).

Your Response

Is there anything in today's reflection that felt like a specific grace given to you? Explore this with Jesus in your prayer or journaling.

Your fellow traveler,
Liena

"Feed My Sheep!"

God's Beloved,

When we fail at new undertakings, we often go back to what we have known or done before. Some of us go back to relatively healthy things; others fall back into addiction and other unhealthy patterns.

Today we find Peter fishing with his friends after the disappointing and hard events in Jerusalem. Has he abolished the idea of being the fisherman of people and gone back to what he did before meeting Jesus? Most likely.

Jesus does not want to see Peter regress. He comes and looks for His friend. He has words of encouragement for Peter. Might Jesus be looking for you too? What does He want to say to you?

Preparing to Reflect

Among many things, prayer is a state of restorative rest. I come to this time of reflection to be quieted, held, and restored in God's loving presence. I visualize the text from Deuteronomy 33:12, "Let the beloved of the LORD rest secure in him, for he shields him all day long, and the one the LORD loves rests between his shoulders." What would it be like to rest between my Father's shoulders? I take some time to allow myself to be carried in this way.

Prayer

My loving Father, I silently marvel at the love You have for me. I let myself rest between Your shoulders as You carry me. Amen.

Story of the Day

Afterward Jesus appeared again to his disciples, by the Sea of Galilee.

It happened this way: Simon Peter, Thomas (also known as Didymus), Nathanael from Cana in Galilee, the sons of Zebedee, and two other disciples were together. "I'm going out to fish," Simon Peter told them, and they said, "We'll go with you." So they went out and got into the boat, but that night they caught nothing.

Early in the morning, Jesus stood on the shore, but the disciples did not realize that it was Jesus.

He called out to them, "Friends, haven't you any fish?"

"No," they answered.

He said, "Throw your net on the right side of the boat and you will find some." When they did, they were unable to haul the net in because of the large number of fish.

Then the disciple whom Jesus loved said to Peter, "It is the Lord!" As soon as Simon Peter heard him say, "It is the Lord," he wrapped his outer garment around him (for he had taken it off) and jumped into the water. The other disciples followed in the boat, towing the net full of fish, for they were not far from shore, about a hundred yards. When they landed, they saw a fire of burning coals there with fish on it, and some bread.

Jesus said to them, "Bring some of the fish you have just caught." So Simon Peter climbed back into the boat and dragged the net ashore. It was full of large fish, 153, but even with so many the net was not torn. Jesus said to them, "Come and have breakfast." None of the disciples dared ask him, "Who are you?" They knew it was the Lord. Jesus came, took the bread and gave it to them, and did the same with the fish. This was now the third time Jesus appeared to his disciples after he was raised from the dead.

When they had finished eating, Jesus said to Simon Peter, "Simon son of John, do you love me more than these?"

"Yes, Lord," he said, "you know that I love you."

Jesus said, "Feed my lambs."

Again Jesus said, "Simon son of John, do you love me?"

He answered, "Yes, Lord, you know that I love you."

Jesus said, "Take care of my sheep."

The third time he said to him, "Simon son of John, do you love me?" Peter was hurt because Jesus asked him the third time, "Do you love me?" He said, "Lord, you know all things; you know that I love you."

Jesus said, "Feed my sheep. Very truly I tell you, when you were younger you dressed yourself and went where you wanted; but when you are old you will stretch out your hands, and someone else will dress you and lead you where you do not want to go." Jesus said this to indicate the kind of death by which Peter would glorify God. Then he said to him, "Follow me!"

Peter turned and saw that the disciple whom Jesus loved was following them. (This was the one who had leaned back against Jesus at the supper and had said, "Lord, who is going to betray you?") When Peter saw him, he asked, "Lord, what about him?"

Jesus answered, "If I want him to remain alive until I return, what is that to you? You must follow me." Because of this, the rumor spread among the believers that this disciple would not die. But Jesus did not say that he would not die; he only said, "If I want him to remain alive until I return, what is that to you?"

This is the disciple who testifies to these things and who wrote them down. We know that his testimony is true.

Jesus did many other things as well. If every one of them were written down, I suppose that even the whole world would not have room for the books that would be written (John 21:1-25).

Entering the Scene

Do you recognize this scene? It's almost an exact replica of Jesus' first meeting with Peter! Peter met Jesus on a day when our Lord was preaching to a huge crowd on the shore by the Sea of Galilee. Jesus approached Peter and asked if He could sit in his fishing boat offshore to address the people. Peter agreed. At the conclusion of His sermon, Jesus prompted Peter, "Put out into deep water, and let down the nets for a catch" (Luke 5:4). The nets were so full that Peter had to call for help to bring in all the fish! At that moment Peter's eyes were open to Jesus' holiness. Jesus kept encouraging Peter, "Don't be afraid; from now on you will fish for people" (Luke 5:10). That was how Peter and Jesus first met.

Now it happens all over again. Jesus comes at dawn. He finds his friends discouraged over having not caught any fish, and He directs them to throw their empty nets on the other side of the boat to haul in a huge catch. *It is the intention of Jesus to forge a connection in Peter's mind—to help Peter reestablish his identity as a fisher of men.*

As they are throwing the net, John suddenly stops. The familiarity of the atmosphere and movements shocks him. He listens to the sudden revelation and exclaims, "It is the Lord!" Upon hearing John's shout of joy and surprise, Peter grabs his outer garments. Is Peter still trying to cover his shame? Only then Peter dives into the water and swims to the shore.

Take a look at Jesus' expression right now. Is Jesus' face sunlit with a luminous smile as He watches His passionate disciple swimming toward Him?

Peter walks, soaking wet, from the lake and finds a fire and a loving meal prepared by Jesus. What is this moment of reunion like for Peter and Jesus?

The other disciples row in the boat sinking low from the load of fish. The warmth of sweltering coals welcomes them in the chilly morning. Jesus stirs the campfire and says, "Bring some of the fish you have just caught."

Peter plunges back into the water to help drag ashore a net crowded with fish! Can you hear the fish flapping all over while the disciples sit down to enjoy Jesus' cooking? The disciples' emotions are almost bursting with suppressed and giggly joy like an overinflated balloon. None of the disciples dare to ask Jesus, "Who are You?"

What do they talk about? Imagine dining with these men and receiving fish and bread from Jesus' hand. How do you find yourself in their company?

After the breakfast, Jesus asks Peter to walk with Him. Watch them moving along the lake shore. What do you see?

Going Deeper

The Greek language has four words for love.[5] *Storge*—the love that family members feel for one another. *Phileo*—the loyal love shared by good friends. Eros—the love experienced by lovers. And *Agape*—the the highest and most sacrificial form of love.

The first two times Jesus asks Peter, "Peter, do you truly *agape* me?" I wonder if Peter hesitated before replying. "Lord, you know all things; you know that I *phileo* you." Notice that Peter uses a different word for love than Jesus does. He is honest that *phileo* is the best he can do. The third time Jesus honors Peter's honesty and quietly asks, "Do you *phileo* me?" No shaming! With each question Jesus led Peter on a journey of truly examining his heart and naming the truth within. Do you have friends that ask good questions and challenge you to be truthful with yourself?

Besides giving Peter the opportunity to examine the truth of his own heart, Jesus was also giving Peter the chance to affirm his love for the Lord—three times to replace his three-fold denial. And all three times, Jesus reenlists Peter to lead His church. "Peter, feed my sheep." Can you envision Peter's shock? In what ways does the Lord help you to reinstate your true identity and dignity?

When Jesus asks the third time if Peter loves Him, Peter is overcome by sadness. Does he wonder whether Jesus is worried that given the right set of circumstances Peter will repeat his denials? Is this why Jesus follows each request by renewing His call to leadership? Jesus is building confidence in Peter's heart as He repeats, "Feed my lambs. . . Take care of my sheep. . . .Feed my sheep. Very truly I tell you, when you were younger you dressed yourself and went where you wanted; but when you are olsd you will stretch out your hands, and someone else will dress you and lead you where you do not want to go" (John 21:15-18). Jesus said this to indicate the kind of death by which Peter would glorify God. Then He said to him, "Follow me!"

In a single stroke, Jesus confronts Peter's fear and assures him that in the future he would *not* repeat the same mistake. Peter would never again deny Jesus and run.

Peter's insecurity is hard to dislodge. When Peter sees John following behind them, he makes a comment that exposes his insecurity, "Lord, what about him?" It's easy to see how Peter would be toying with the question. Jesus, isn't John better qualified to lead Your people? John didn't deny You as I did. *Wouldn't You be better off with someone more reliable?* When have you felt similar in your walk with the Lord?

Jesus sternly replies that John has his own work to do. Isn't this stunning? So many of us rejoice in having been forgiven, yet we persist in the conviction that our flaws and failings disqualify us from service. Jesus arranges this lake encounter specifically and intentionally to correct this misunderstanding in Peter's life and also in our lives. Note, that Jesus never questions Peter's skill set to reinstate him in ministry. Instead the Lord speaks *only* about Peter's *quality of love* in a way that motivates his desire to love Jesus even more.

By the end of their walk on the lakeshore, Jesus had offered Peter the same invitation He had extended in their first meeting, "Peter, follow Me!" Then Jesus gives Peter work to do, "Feed My sheep."

In the same way, Jesus questions us today, "Do you truly love Me?" Then look after the people you meet as a shepherd would care for his beloved sheep!

Impressions of Jesus' Heart for Your Journey

Above all things, pray that you would love Me deeply. Love for Me is the foundation of your faith. Without love everything crumbles. "Love the Lord your God with all your heart and with all your soul and with all your strength and with all your mind'; and, 'Love your neighbor as yourself" (Luke10:27).

Your Response

What is your heart's response to today's reflection? Express yourself to Jesus.

> *May the Lord smile on you,*
> *Your friend.*
> *Liena*

Falling in Love

My Friend,

Together we have arrived at the last devotional for this Lent season. Thank you from the depth of my heart for coming all the way with me on this journey. Before we say goodbye, I would like to share with you how God called me to write and how this devotional found a way to you. I hope that my story will serve as an encouragement to you.

I grew up in Latvia, Eastern Europe. All my elementary school years I struggled with writing, particularly with grammar. The vicious struggle stifled my ability to write. The writer in me was "wrapped up in graveclothes" like Lazarus and put away in "the grave" until God gave me a prophetic word many years later.

Over ten years ago I was going through a very hard season in my life. I happened to be in Denver one Sunday morning and walked into an unknown church. During the extended praise and worship the pastor walked up to me. She lifted my chin and said, "Sharpen your pencil. God wants you to write." Tears started to stream down my cheeks, and I hid these words like a treasure deeply in my heart. For the longest time I did not know what to write.

Many years passed again until my close friend, Jacqueline, came to visit me for Christmas. We prayed together each morning using a prayer method inspired by St. Ignatius. Here are the steps we took each time we prayed together:

• Preparing to Reflect and Pray.

We chose a Bible text and started with silence and recollection of ourselves before the presence of God.

• Seeking the Holy Spirit's Guidance.

Jacqueline and I asked the Holy Spirit to illuminate the Scriptures and our own hearts.

• Engaging the Imagination.

We slowly read the Scripture for the first time and used all our senses to enter the scene depicted in the passage. We allowed God to use our imagination to connect with the real life of His Word. Jacqueline and I discussed what we felt and perceived.

• Engaging the Heart and Intellect.

Next, we read the Scripture slowly for the second time and paid attention to words, phrases, and God's deeper message to us. We shared our impressions with each other.

• Praying the Scripture.

We prayed very specifically for the new revelations to take root in our hearts and shape our lives. We permitted the Scriptures to form and shape our prayers.

Later, after Jacqueline returned home, we prayed faithfully in the same way over the phone for about a year until I heard God speaking again into my spirit, "I want you to invite others into your prayer circle." I asked "How, Lord?" The answer was, "Write!"

Here it was; the initial assignment. That's how our first book, *Advent to Epiphany: Engaging the Heart of Christmas*, came to be. This devotional is a natural continuation to the Advent devotional. Even though Jacqueline could not be part of creating this second gift to you, my good friend Miriam Dixon has had a very important part in birthing this book.

While fashioning this devotional, my deepest desire has been that you would fall in the love with the Lord, and if you already have, that you would deepen this love until all doubt about His affection toward you is naturally incapacitated and dismissed. I have prayed that gratitude, wonder, astonishment, and praise would occupy the inner territory of your heart. I can't find better words for my farewell than Fr. Pedro Arrupe's prayerful encouragement:

Nothing is more practical than
finding God, than
falling in Love
in a quite absolute, final way.
What you are in love with,
what seizes your imagination, will affect everything.
It will decide
what will get you out of bed in the morning,
what you do with your evenings,
how you spend your weekends,
what you read, whom you know,
what breaks your heart,
and what amazes you with joy and gratitude.
Fall in Love, stay in love,
and it will decide everything.[6]

Indeed and forever,
Your friend Liena

_____

_____

_____

_____

_____

_____

_____

_____

_____

_____

_____

_____

_____

_____

_____

_____

_____

_____

_____

_____

_____

_____

_____

_____

Endnotes

The First Week of Lent

[1] Antonio T. De Nicolas, *Powers Of Imagining: Ignatius De Loyola* (Albany, State University of New York Press, 1986), 164.

[2] Dallas Willard, *Hearing God: Developing a Conversational Relationship with God* (Downer Grove, IVP Books, 2012), 227.

[3] Willard, 228.

[4] E. Stanley Jones, *A Song of Ascents: A Spiritual Autobiography* (Nashville, Abingdon Press, 1979), 190.

[5] Willard, 230.

[6] *Goodreads*, https://www.goodreads.com/ quotes/220038-the-present-state-of-the-world-and-the-whole-of.

[7] Andrew Murray, *The Indwelling Spirit: The Work of the Holy Spirit in the Life of the Believer* (Minneapolis, Bethany House, 2006), 15.

[8] Henri Nouwen, "Brining the Spirit Through Leaving", *Henri Nouwen Society*, https://henrinouwen.org/meditation/bringing-spirit-leaving.

[9] "The Prayer of Saint Patrick", *Journey with Jesus*, www.journeywithjesus.net poemsandprayers/668-saint-patrick-prayer.

[10] Murray, 81.

[11] Murray, 82.

[12] Fr.Richard Rohr, "The Communion of Saints", *Center for Action and Contemplation*, https://cac.org/the-communion-of-saints-2016-12-14/.

[13] Carlo Carretto, "The God Who Comes", *Oratio Contamplativa*, https://oratiocontemplativa.wordpress.com/2013/06/28/ democracy-of-the-dead-carlo-carretto/.

[14] Graham Cooke,"God is not a Visitor", *Brilliant Perspectives*, http://brilliant-perspectives.com/god-not-visitor.

[15] Andrew Murray, *The Practice of God's Presence* (New Kensington, Whitaker House, 2000), 256.

[16] Cynthia Bourgeault, *The Wisdom Way of Knowing: Reclaiming An Ancient Tradition to Awaken the Heart* (San Francisco, Josey-Bass, 2003), 74, 75.

[17] Bishop Kallistos-Ware, "Prayer and Silence", *Prayer and Silence*, www.ortho-doxprayer.org/Articles_files/Ware-1%20Prayer%20and%20Silence.html.

[18] Ralph Milton, *The Essence of Julian: A Paraphrase of Julian of Norwich's "Revelations of Divine Love"* (Chico, Northstone, 2002), 23.

[19] Allison Bown, "The Language of an Overcomer", *Training Journal For Warriors, Champions & Game Changers,* www.twclass.org/wp-content/uploads/2016/09/training_journal_14_2015-03.pdf.

[20] Graham Cooke, "The Importance of The Fruits of the Spirit", *In Focus,* https://infocuswithteambrilliant.wordpress.com/2015/12/22/the-importance-and-existence-of-the-fruits-of-the-spirit/.

[21] St. John of Kronstadt, *OrthodoxWiki,* http://www.peterandpaul.net/Quote-stjohnkronstadtprayingalone.

[22] "Latvia", *World War II,* https://ww2db.com/country/Latvia.

[23] "Siberian Exile—Life in 'Resettlement' Camps and the GULAG," *latvians. com,* https://latvians.com/index.php?en/Exile/Siberia/index.ssi). Departed to Siberia – Latvian.

The Second Week of Lent

[1] Howard Thurman, *Meditations of the Heart* (Boston, Beacon Press, 1999), 28.

[2] Eugene H. Peterson, *As Kingfishers Catch Fire—A Conversation on the Ways of God Formed by the Words of God,* (New York, WaterBrook, 2017), page numbe340.

[3] Peterson, 340,341.

[4] Rainer Maria Rilke, *Goodreads,* www.goodreads.com/quotes/717-be-patient-toward-all-that-is-unsolved-in-your-heart.

[5] "Bible Commentaries", *Studylight.org, Clarke's Notes on the Bible,* www.study-light.org/bible/cjb/john/14-27.html.

[6] M. Henry, "Christ's Legacy", *Bible Hub,* https://biblehub.com/sermons/auth/henry/christ's_legacy.htm.

[7] Cynthia Bourgeault, *Mystical Hope: Trusting in the Mercy of God* (Lanham, Crowley Publications, 2001), 9-10.

[8] Hesychasm-The Practice of Silence, *SCRBD,* www.scribd.com/document/256534071/Hesychasm-The-Practice-of-Silence.

[9] Graham Cooke, "Joy Is Who God Is", *Brilliant Perspectives,* http://brilliantper-spectives.com/joy-is-who-god-is/.

[10] Sermon by John MacArthur, "The Lord's Greatest Prayer," *Grace to You,* www.gty.org/library/sermons-library/43-93/the-lords-greatest-prayer-part-1.

[11] MacArthur.

[12] Prayer Coach, "40 More Prayer Quotes by Graham Cooke", *Grace to You,* https://prayer-coach.com/2013/03/07/prayer-quotes-graham-cooke-2/.

[13] Graham Cooke, *Crafted Prayer* (Vacaville, Brilliant Book House, 2004), 13.

[14] Frederica Mathewes-Green, *The Jesus Prayer: The Ancient Desert Prayer that Tunes the Heart to God* (Brewster, Paraclete Press, 2009), 13.

[15] C. Baxter Kruger, *The Great Dance: The Christian Vision Revisited* (Vancouver, Regent College Publishing, 2005), 22.

[16] Kruger, 23.

[17] Mark Batterson, Parker Batterson, *The Grave Robber: How Jesus Can Make Your Impossible Possible* (Grand Rapids, Baker Books, Student edition, 2015), 149.

[18] Batterson, 153,154.

[19] Christopher J. Wiles, "Death Working Backwards": Narnia, Deeper Magic, and Easter, www.thornscompose.com/2010/03/25/death-working-backwards-narnia-deeper-magic-and-easter.

[20] Caryll Houselander, *The Way of the Cross* (Liguori, Liguori Publications, 2002), 39.

[21] Brian Tidd

[22] Fr. Richard Rohr, "Knowing through Loving", *Center for Action and Contemplation*, https://cac.org/knowing-through-loving 2017-02-26/.

[23] Jacques Philippe, *Thirsting for Prayer* (Burtin, Scepter Publishers, 2014), 56.

The Third Week of Lent

[1] John van de Laar, "Call For Allegiance", *Sacredise*, http://sacredise.com/prayers/season/holy-week/calls-for-allegiance/.

[2] Jacques Philippe, *In the School of the Holy Spirit* (New York, Scepter Publishers, 2007), 88.

[3] Philippe, 88.

[4] Albert Day, *The Captivating Presence: A Minister's Intimate Interaction with God* (Atlanta, Enthea Press, 2001), 99.

[5] Msgr. Charles Pope, "The Bread of Affliction: A Meditation on What Jesus Endured at the Last Supper," *Community in Mission*, http://blog.adw.org/2015/04/the-bread-of-affliction-a-meditation-on-what-jesus-endured-at-the-last-supper.

[6] Pope.

[7] Fr Richard Rohr, "Eucharist", *Richard Rohr's Daily Meditation,* http://myemail.constantcontact.com/Richard-Rohr-s-Meditation--Take--Thank--Break--Give.html?soid=1103098668616&aid=WjWZtMC8GNE.

[8] Dr. Paul Brand and Philip Yancey, *In His Image* (Grand Rapids, Zondervan, 2009), 820-827.

[9] Fr Richard Foster, "The Prayer of Relinquishment", *Greg Nettle blog*, http://gregnettle.blogspot.com/2007/01/prayer-of-relinquishment.html.

[10] Michael Casey, Fully Human, Fully Divine: An Intractive Christology (Liguori, 2004), 251.

[11] Casey, 255.

[12] Casey, 264.

[13] Houselander, 3.

[14] Joseph Scriven, "What a Friend We Have in Jesus," 1855.

[15] Houselander, 72.

[16] Robert Farrar Capon, *Kingdom, Grace, Judgment: Paradox, Outrage, and Vindication in the Parables of Jesus* (Grand Rapids, Wm. B. Eerdmans, 2002), 19.

[17] Mathewes-Green, 91.

[18] Graham Cooke, "God Is Present-Future", *In Focus*, https://infocuswith-teambrilliant.wordpress.com/2016/01/18/god-is-present-future/.

[19] Michael Downey, "On Learning How To Look", (Weavings: A Journal Of The Christian Spiritual Life, Nashville, The Upper Room, Vol. XXVI, No.4), 29.

[20] Downey, 28-29.

The Fourth Week of Lent

[1] Graham Cooke, "The Constancy of God", *In Focus,* https://infocuswith-teambrilliant.wordpress.com/2012/11/19/131/.

[2] Day, 57-58.

[3] Ray S. Anderson, *Judas and Jesus* (Eugene, Cascade Books, 2005), 9.

[4] Graham Cooke, *The Nature of God: Upgrading Your Image Of God And Who He Wants To Be For You* (Tonbridge, Sovereign World, 2003), 9.

[5] "A Prayer for Holy Monday", *The Lutheran Church-Missouri Synod*, https://plus.google.com/+lutheranchurchmissourisynod.

[6] Fenelon, *The Seeking Heart* (Jacksonville, SeedSowers, 1992), 6.

[7] Houselander, 34.

[8] Mathewes-Green, 40.

[9] Arthur W. Pink, *The Seven Sayings of the Savior on the Cross* (The Ephesians Four Group, 2017),494.

[10] Pink, 574.

[11] Fr.John-Julian, *Paraclete Giants: The Complete Julian of Norwich,* (Brewster, Paraclete Press, 2009), 335.

[12] Fr. John-Julian, 147.

[13] O. Hallesby, "PRAYER: The Breath of the Soul", *The Value of Sparrows,* https://thevalueofsparrows.com/2012/02/16/prayer-the-breath-of-the-soul-by-ole-hallesby/.

[14] Houselander, 90.

[15] Pink, 808.
[16] Pink, 920.
[17] Houselander, 72-73.
[18] Mathewes-Green, 139-140.
[19] Michael H. Crosby, *The Seven Last Words* (New York, Orbis books, 1994), 531-532.
[20] Mathewes-Green, 141.

The Fifth Week of Lent

[1] "Saint Teresa of Calcutta", *franciscanmedia.org*, https://info.franciscanmedia.org/mother-teresa-old.
[2] "I Thirst For You"-A Letter From Mother Teresa", *Catholic Link,* https://catholic-link.org/quotes/i-thirst-letter-written-mother-teresa-quote/.
[3] "What was the Roman practice of disposing of dead bodies?, Biblical Hermeneutics beta, https://hermeneutics.stackexchange.com/questions/27747/what-was-the-roman-practice-for-disposing-of-dead-bodies.
[4] Aleteia, https://aleteia.org/2018/04/01/do-not-abandon-yourselves-to-despair-we-are-the-easter-people-and-hallelujah-is-our-song/.
[5] "Call to Worship: Amen! Amen! Amen!", *re:Worship,* https://re-worship.blogspot.com/2015/10/call-to-worship-amen-amen-amen.html.
[6] Richard Rohr, "Jesus' Bodily Resurrection", *Center for Action and Contemplation,* https://cac.org/jesus-bodily-resurrection-2018-04-01/.
[7] Robert Fulghum, *It Was On Fire When I Lay Down On It* (New York, Random House, 1988, 1989), 174.
[8] Daily Encouragement Net, "A Prayer For Running The Race", VERSE365.COM, http://verse365.com/page/221/.

Unfolding Resurrection

[1] Tilden Edwards, *Living In The Presence: Spiritual Exercises to Open Our Lives to the Awareness of God* (New York, HarperCollins, 1995), 11.
[2] Ruth Haley Barton, *Life Together in Christ: Experiencing Transformation in Community* (Downers Grove, IVP Books, 2014), 26.
[3] Edwards, 2.
[4] Barton, 140-141.
[5] Wikipedia, The Free Encyclopedia, https://en.wikipedia.org/wiki/Greek_words_for_love.
[6] From *Finding God in All Things: A Marquette Prayer Book* © 2009 Marquette University. Used with permission.